Franco Nardini

Technical Progress and Economic Growth

Business Cycles and Stabilization Policies

Springer

Author

Prof. Franco Nardini
Department of Mathematics
for Economics and Social Sciences
University of Bologna
Viale Q. Filopanti, 5
40126 Bologna, Italy

Cataloging-in-Publication data applied for

Die Deutsche Bibliothek - CIP-Einheitsaufnahme

Nardini, Franco:
Technical progress and economic growth : business cycles and
stabilization policies / Franco Nardini. - Berlin ; Heidelberg ; New
York ; Barcelona ; Hong Kong ; London ; Milan ; Paris ; Singapore ;
Tokyo : Springer, 2001
  (Lecture notes in economics and mathematical systems ; 500)
  ISBN 3-540-41596-3

ISSN 0075-8450
ISBN 3-540-41596-3 Springer-Verlag Berlin Heidelberg New York

Springer-Verlag Berlin Heidelberg New York
a member of BertelsmannSpringer Science+Business Media GmbH

© Springer-Verlag Berlin Heidelberg 2001
Printed in Germany

Typesetting: Camera ready by author
Printed on acid-free paper   SPIN: 10795437   55/3142/du   5 4 3 2 1 0

Lecture Notes in Economic and Mathematical Systems

Founding Editors:

M. Beckmann
H. P. Künzi

Managing Editors:

Prof. Dr. G. Fandel
Fachbereich Wirtschaftswissenschaften
Fernuniversität Hagen
Feithstr. 140/AVZ II, 58084 Hagen, Germany

Prof. Dr. W. Trockel
Institut für Mathematische Wirtschaftsforschung (IMW)
Universität Bielefeld
Universitätsstr. 25, 33615 Bielefeld, Germany

Co-Editors:

C. D. Aliprantis, Dan Kovenock

Springer
*Berlin
Heidelberg
New York
Barcelona
Hong Kong
London
Milan
Paris
Singapore
Tokyo*

to Alessandra

Preface

In this book we intend to discuss economic fluctuations and growth and possible stabilizing fiscal policies. Since these topics are major preoccupations of economic theorists and have been extensively discussed since the classics, one may wonder why another book on these subjects. A possible defense is that we are going to do so in the framework of a two-sector model where the main features of each sector depend on the characteristics of the goods produced by the sector itself.

The conventional wisdom suggests that the problem of (dis)aggregation in growth and business cycle theory is basically a quantitative one: the model should consider as many sectors, goods, and agents as necessary to provide a sufficiently rich picture, the upper bound obviously resulting from the tractability of the problem. In this attitude the same equilibrium (or disequilibrium) assumptions generally hold true throughout all sectors.

Here we want to prove the relevance of an alternative approach: we look at the qualitative differences across sectors and at the peculiarities of each market as at the determinants of the economic dynamics. This tradition goes back over one hundred years to Tugan-Baranowkj and has been developed by Aftalion, Fanno, Spiethof, and Lowe, but has never been systematically formalized. To do so we revisit the polarity between fix-price and flex-price markets discussed at length by Hicks; in this view price and quantity adjustments may cohabit or alternate in the same market, since the functioning of the market depend on the goods traded. Thus the sectors of our model are asymmetric and irregular endogenous business cycles perturb the growth trend as a result of these asymmetries, the different impact of technical progress across different sectors, and the lack of coordination in the lengthy process of capital accumulation in each of them.

We examine labor saving and capital saving technical progresses in each sector separately, discussing the conditions in which they result in an expansion stimulus and when the opposite holds and they prime an overproduction crisis.

We discuss various alternative options of fiscal policy in order to determine what the government might and should do either to avert a recession and support activity levels or to cool down aggregate demand, when the pace of economic growth quickens and the rate of inflation rises.

The book ends with an extension of the model to a case of open economy: a large advanced country exports capital goods in a smaller developing one, importing consumption goods. We address the problem of stabilizing the economy of the large country together with the conditions allowing a successful industrialization process in the small one.

This book is divided into four parts.

In the first part we present our model and discuss its features comparing them to those already preset in the literature.

In the second part we describe the equilibria of the system, the growth in equilibrium, the dynamics far from equilibrium, and the effects of technical progress on the evolution of the system.

In the third part we aim at providing some results to the long lasting debate on the effectiveness of fiscal policy to stabilize the economic system.

In the fourth part the model is extended in order to deal with an open economy which exports capital goods and imports consumption goods.

In particular chapter 1 provides an overview of many two- three- and multi-sector model, discusses their main features and compares them to those of our model.

In chapter 2 we give a complete description of the main assumptions underlying our model with particular emphasis on the aforementioned qualitative differences in the market structures and the induced different organization of each sector.

In chapter 3 we introduce the main variables of the model and provide a formalization of the assumptions introduced in chapter 2. Since markets do not need to be always in equilibrium, we describe the reactions of agents to the emergence of disequilibria and their impact on production, investment, and prices; further we discuss when rationing occurs and when profit falls in one or in both sectors.

In chapter 4 we give a detailed description of the dynamical system in all the aforementioned situations, analyzing the evolution of the demand, production, and investment in each of them.

We pass to part 2 with chapter 5 where we prove that the model has multiple equilibria and that they are generally unstable, so that the economy may either fall into a depression phase or accelerate toward an overheating regime.

In chapter 6 we describe the evolution of the depression and the overproduction crisis which concludes it; then we pass to the overheating, showing that in both cases a turning point is reached without assuming any exogenous input to the system.

In chapter 7 we discuss different types of technical progress both in the consumption goods sector and in the capital goods sector. We show that even if technical progress generally has an expansive effect, this may be not the case if pessimistic expectations prevail; in this case the outcome may be an overproduction crisis.

Chapter 8 begins the third part stating the assumptions on the role of the government in the model.

Chapter 9 provides a formal description of the system when the government intervenes issuing taxes, buying goods on the market, supporting households' income by direct transfers.

In chapter 10 we discuss the existence of equilibria and show that they exist provided that the government balances its budget; we also describe the dynamics of the system in a neighborhood of the equilibria.

In chapter 11 we examine how the government may fight inflation rising taxes: we review different forms of consumption and profit taxes.

In chapter 12 expansionary policies are discussed: we examine both tax reductions and increases of direct transfers to households and find conditions for the effectiveness of these strategies.

Part 4 extends the model to describe a large advanced country exporting capital goods and importing consumption goods from a small backward one.

Chapter 13 provides a description of the conditions allowing the beginning and the continuation of an industrialization process in a small backward country; the technological gap is overcome importing capital goods from the advanced country in order to generate a flow of export of consumption goods.

Chapter 14 is devoted to the extension of the model to the case of two countries importing end exporting from one another. We show that two phases may be distinguished in the industrialization process: early phase and further phase.

In chapter 15 the early phase of industrialization is examined and conditions for a successful transition to the further phase are discussed.

The further phase is then analyzed in chapter 16: in particular we discuss how the government of the large country can stabilize the economy contrasting both the intrinsic instability and the perturbations caused by the ongoing industrialization of the small country.

Chapter 17 discusses some open problems.

We have gathered proofs and calculations in a set of appendices at the end of the book.

Acknowledgements

It is a pleasure for the author to acknowledge his debt first and foremost to
G. Gozzi, who has stimulated him to approach the problems treated in this
book, to R. Scazzieri for his invaluable advice and fruitful discussions, to
G. Candela, H. Hagemann, S. Zamagni and all the participants to the sem-
inars held in Bologna, Catania, Cambridge, Genova, Padenghe, Stuttgart,
Trento, Urbino for comments, suggestions and constructive criticism on
preliminary drafts of the book. The usual *caveat* applies.

Contents

II Growth and Business Cycles   43

Part I

A Two-Sector Disequilibrium Model

This part is devoted to the presentation, the construction, the description, and the discussion of our model.

We introduce the presentation by a short overview of some classes of well known models and their main assumptions, in order to set our model in the right perspective (chapter 1). Then we pass to a detailed description of our hypotheses (chapter 2) and their formalization (chapter 3).

We end this part with a complete description of the dynamical system in the different conditions that the economy may experience when the steady state growth path breaks down and oscillations drive the system far from equilibrium positions (chapter 4).

1 Two Three and Multisector Models in the Economic Literature

Two three and multisector models have a well established tradition in economic theory and they have been repeatedly used to deal with problems pertaining to the theory of value, relative prices, distribution and growth, short and long run consequences of exogenous shocks, interindustrial coordination and competition problems.

Obviously the number of different sectors to be included in the model depends on the level of aggregation required by problems the model aims to tackle and not all levels of aggregation are equally suitable for the study of all problems. It is in the nature of relative prices as a set of exchange ratios between individual commodities that interdependence of such prices can be adequately depicted only in a model as high disaggregated as the Walrasian.

Subject of this book is the theory of growth and the business cycle, which concerns matter as building and wearing down of fixed capital, the accumulation and decumulation of inventories, and the flow of input and output. The appropriate level of aggregation is, therefore, much higher since all these macroeconomic issues are practically independent of individual units[1].

Obviously the number of sectors is not the only possible way of classifying multisector models; instead of the level of aggregation we may choose the alternative criterium of classifying them according to, say, the method of

---

[1]For an comprehensive discussion on these points we refer to Lowe (1976) Introduction.

aggregation. Sectors may be either vertically integrated[2] or horizontally aggregated[3]; clearly many different intermediate solutions[4] are possible[5].

The former description generally aims at highlighting problems of competition among different sector, whereas the last one is designed to treat the interplay of different industrial sectors at different stages of the production process.

Since the problems we are going to address are the accumulation of fixed capital in each sector, the possible emergence of disproportions due to the length of this process and coordination problems that arise in such contest, we are led to choose an horizontal aggregation, which will allow us to describe the productive process as a sequence of successive interconnected phases: investment decisions, production and installation of capital goods, production decisions in the consumption goods sector, supply and price decisions in the consumption goods market.

The aim of this chapter is to briefly review different classes of multisectorial models with a well established tradition in economic literature. This short survey allows us to introduce our model and discuss its relation with the other ones. In the following chapter we present the detailed assumptions of our model and their critical discussion.

1.1   Multisector models and dynamic analysis

Dynamic multisector models may be grouped into five classes:

1. Leontief's dynamic model and its generalizations;

2. multisector neo-classical models;

3. classical-Marxian dynamic models of gravitation;

4. traverse models;

5. structural theories of the business cycles[6].

The dynamics characterizing each class of models does emphasize different aspects of the real dynamic mechanisms at work in a capitalist (or market) economy.

---

[2] See for instance Pasinetti (1993).

[3] See for instance Uzawa (1961), Hicks (1965), Solow Tobin von Weizaecker and Yaari (1966), Lowe (1976). See also the short survey in Dixit (1976) chapter 6.

[4] See for instance Pasinetti (1981), Kuga (1977).

[5] As correctly observed by Hicks, even the degree of integration of real economic systems may considerably vary from one system to the other and through time (see Hicks (1973) Chapter 1 § 3).

[6] Here we adopt the terminology of Hagemann and Landesmann (1996).

1.1.1   The dynamic Leontief model

Input-output dynamic models describe the evolution of prices and quantities according to a dynamical process that is characterized by the following set of assumptions: fixed coefficients production function, full utilization of the productive capacity of each sector within each period; a uniform rate of profit across sectors in each period and not asymptotically as the result of capital mobility across sectors as in the classical and Marxian analysis of gravitation, i.e. of the stability of long-term equilibrium.

On the quantity side the assumption of full capacity utilization implies that the investment function is linear and of the acceleration type; concerning prices the model assumes a condition of uniform rate of profit across sectors within each period by taking into account explicitly capital gains and/or losses, i.e. by assuming perfect foresight. It is by now well known that this type of dynamic model is characterized by the so-called dual instability property; relative stability of the quantity path implies instability of the price path and vice-versa[7].

Here we want to stress one point: the Leontief dynamic model assumes that within each period markets for commodities are in equilibrium and therefore it belongs to the class of equilibrium dynamics models. Furthermore it considers only the case of full capacity utilization along the dynamic path followed by the economy. As Aoki[8] has aptly and convincingly pointed out, the unstable dynamics that characterizes the Leontief model is a direct consequence of this assumption. Our model, on the contrary, assumes a variable degree of utilization of productive capacity in both sectors[9], and the possibility of rationing concerning the decisions of production and investment.

1.1.2   Neo-classical multisector models

Neo-classical multisector dynamic models describe the dynamics of the capitalist economy as a sequence of temporary equilibria[10]. This type of models is meant mainly to generalize the Meade-Samuelson-Solow-Swan parables[11]

---

[7]For a proof of this result and a comprehensive overview of this problem we refer to Burmeister and Dobell (1970), Morishima (1964), Morishima (1969), Jorgenson (1961), Woods (1978).

[8]In his fundamental contribution, Aoki (1977). On this point an interesting analysis is developed by Fukuoka (1977).

[9]Or, to put the same thing in different words, in our model the degree of capacity utilisation is an endogenous variable.

[10]Important contributions are, among the others Hahn (1966), Kurz (1968), Cass and Shell (1976), Kuga (1977), Burmeister Dobell Caton and Ross (1973). This list is, of course, not exhaustive.

A good survey of the literature may be found in Burmeister (1980), chapter 6.

[11]See Swan (1956), Meade (1961), Samuelson (1962), Solow (1965).

of aggregate models of growth lead by accumulation of capital and increasing population to the more realistic case of a multi-sector, multi-commodity world. These models make explicit the basic structure of growth theory; from the neo-classical (i.e. marginalist) point of view growth theory is considered as the extension of the theory of general economic equilibrium to the intertemporal context. The main aspects that is worth stressing are the following.

1. The multisector neo-classical model does not consider an autonomous investment function[12]; investment adjusts passively to the existing volume of savings. As is well known things work well in the aggregate model and in two-sector models à la Uzawa for one simple reason: in such models there exists just one way to keep one's wealth, the stock of the unique capital good. Things are different in the multisector model; when several capital goods are taken into account there is a problem of portfolio equilibrium on the part of the capitalists when deciding how to invest their savings.

2. A uniform rate of profit prevails within each period for the class of models we are considering; this equal remuneration of invested capital is obtained through changing price expectations. In this type of models the price system does fulfil two tasks, equating demand and supply on the markets and establishing a uniform profitability for wealth's investors. This requires as almost necessary to formulate assumptions concerning price expectations; within the approach of the formulation of a dynamic equilibrium path it is almost absolutely necessary to assume (at least myopic) perfect foresight. The rate of profit is uniform, in each period while relative prices of goods are changing period after period.

The steady-state for this class of models is a saddle-point; thus the dynamics is divergent, except when the (given) initial conditions for the economy are on the stable manifold. Finally, these models too assume full utilization of productive capacity.

---

[12]This is true, of course, of the aggregate neoclassical model of economic growth. In a sense this is one of the distinguishing features of neoclassical analysis of the working of the capitalist economy in the long run, i.e. the adjustment of investment to savings. Keynesian aspects concerning effective demand are considered to be relevant only in the short period and completely abstracted for in the analysis of the long run evolution of the economy.

1.1.3 Classical models of gravitation

Many economists have bee aware since a long time that the assumption that all markets are in equilibrium at every time may be unrealistic[13]. Thus in the last two decades we have witnessed a renewed interest in the classical analysis of competition for a capitalist economy. According to the classical analysis of competition two mechanisms are at work in the capitalist economy.

1. Capital is allocated to the productive sectors according to profit rate differentials (law of profitability).

2. Prices of commodities change according to disequilibrium on the market (law of demand and supply).

Three types of models[14] have been employed in order to formalize the main aspects of the classical conception of competition for the capitalist economy and to test its relevance, i.e. the gravitation[15] of the economy around a path representing the long-period position (equilibrium) of the economy:

- *models of cross-dual dynamics*[16]. Within this class we may distinguish between:

  - models of complete disequilibrium;
  - models with rationing on the commodity markets.

- *models of sequences of temporary equilibria.*

Classical-Marxian models of gravitation are different in a number of points from the models so far considered.

---

[13] "The fundamental weakeness of the Temporary Equilibrium method is the assumption...that the market is in equilibrium-actual demand equals desired demand, actual supply equals desired supply-even in the *very short* period... In relation to modern manufacturing industry, it is very hard to swallow indeed. Hicks (1965) p. 76.

[14] The literature on the classical analysis of convergence to equilibrium is growing fastly in size. We refer the reader to Dumènil and Lèvy (1989), Dumènil and Lèvy (1993) for a broader perspective on classical economic dynamics and its relevance for understanding the evolution of modern capitalist economies. For a detailed survey of the dynamic models of capitalist competition inspired by the work of the Classics and Marx we refer the reader to Boggio (1993)b and Boggio and Gozzi (1993).

[15] If we abstract from exogenous disturbances of the economy the gravitation problem may be formulated in terms of stability of equilibrium. This is the actual approach taken by the majority of contributions on the matter.

[16] The very name 'cross-dual dynamics' reflects the symmetric effects of the two above mentioned laws: disequilibria on prices (profitability differentials) have an impact on quantities, while disequilibria on quantities affect prices. Thus the law of profitability is to be seen as a cross-dual relationship from prices to quantities, while the law of demand and supply is a relationship from quantities to prices.

The dynamics of the economy is a disequilibrium dynamics which is corrected by the behavior of the agents (firms and capitalists) reacting to the observation of disequilibrium on the markets

Prices of commodities are subject to the law of demand and supply: they increase when the market is characterized by excess demand and decrease in the opposite case. On the other hand capitalists allocate capital (as a sum of purchasing power) according to profit differentials (law of profitability).

The equalization of the rates of profit is obtained asymptotically, i.e. when the dynamic process has fully developed its effects[17] along the transient path the economy is in a state of disequilibrium and therefore rate of profits are not equalized..

Models of complete disequilibrium show another interesting point differentiating them from the preceding models: the degree of capacity utilization may be considered as variable[18].

We are going to modify these assumptions in several points.

First of all in our model the adjustment of the prices of commodities depend on the structure of the market of each commodity and thus may depend not only on excess demand, but also on the existence of inventories.

Second we assume that capitalists do not know the rate of profit of each sector at every time, but they simply observe the rate at which each sector remunerates invested capital.

Obviously when profit in a sector is insufficient to guarantee a suitable remuneration, capitalists move their investment towards the other sector.

When profits are sufficient in both sectors, we assume that the remuneration rates are such that capitalists are indifferent to the sector.

1.1.4   Traverse models

Traverse models are concerned with the problem of transition between long-period positions of the economy as a consequence of structural change. The traverse analysis developed by J. Hicks within a neo-Austrian framework[19] and the model of instrumental analysis of A. Lowe[20] falls within this category.

These models and the term "traverse" itself were introduced by Hicks to highlight the role of technical progress in the growth process of an economy

---

[17] Or, to put it with different words, when the economy has fully adjusted to its long-term equilibrium. See Vianello (1985) for this terminology.

[18] We refer to the contribution Duménil Lévy (1993) both for a thorough discussion on this point and for an introduction to the crucial problem of the stability of a capitalistic economy and the arising of business cycle.

[19] Traverse analysis in a neo-Austrian framework was introduced in Hicks (1973), the term *traverse* appears in Hicks (1965); see also Hicks (1984). We refer the reader to Belloc (1980) and Magnan de Bornier (1980) for developments of the basic model.

[20] See Lowe (1976).

and its structural change. Hicks' model is a dynamic equilibrium model, but not steady state equilibrium one; it assumes that the productive capacity is always fully exploited (see the Hicksian full performance assumption) and describes the production process of a final good in terms of a vertically integrated sector.

Vertical integration is an essential tool for the analysis of short and long run effects of a technical progress; even if technical progresses generally occur in a rather short time, they prime an adaptation process of the productive apparatus that need time and resources in order to fully develope its effects.

Moreover bottlenecks and shortages may emerge during the transition path, due to the age structure of the existing productive capital[21]. Therefore the convergence of the transition path is not to be given for granted, but requires some compatibility conditions to be met[22].

As far as the analytic structure and the degree of aggregation are concerned, Lowe's model is considerably different from Hicks'. Lowe's model is a three sector model based on the postulate of fixed coefficients, with two sectors producing capital goods and a sector producing consumer goods.

However also Lowe's model is concerned with "obstructions of resource shifts, bottlenecks in production, inelasticity in supply owing to the *longue dureé* of capital formation and even more to the large cost of sunk capital" dominating "the adjustment process and, in particular, the adjustment to the major growth stimuli - chance in population, resource supply, and technology"[23].

Also in this model continuous full and efficient utilization of the available resources is assumed in stationary and dynamic equilibria, whereas periods of low utilization of the productive capacity, capital waste, and technological unemployment can not be avoided during some types of traverse[24].

Lowe discusses many types of traverse: adjustment to a different rate of growth of labor supply, adjustment to the dynamics of natural resources supply, and adjustment following the introduction of both labor augmenting and capital augmenting technical innovations.

1.1.5 Structural theories of the business cycles

In the last class of models we gather some theories according to which the cause of periodical crises is to be searched in periods of overproduction, especially in the consumption goods sector; these are in turn due to the different lengths of the production processes in the different sectors of the

---

[21] This is the so called Hayek effect discussed by Zamagni (1984); see also Hageman and Gehrke (1996).

[22] See for instance Nardini (1991) and Nardini (1993).

[23] See Lowe (1976) p. 9

[24] See Lowe (1976) chapter 18 and 24 respectively.

economic system and to the disproportions among different sector, caused by these different lengths.

Among these theories we want to cite and briefly summarize those due to Tugan-Baranowski[25], Fanno[26], and Hicks[27]. In all of them the overproduction, caused by the lag separating the decision to invest in order to increase the output and the actual beginning of the productive life of new plants, appears as an excess supply of consumption goods, that leads to increasing involuntary stockpiling. We cite also Aftalion's theory[28]; in it Say's law is assumed to hold in the aggregate, thus the overproduction causes an immediate fall of prices, that jeopardizes the profitability of firms cramping the capital accumulation process.

In Fanno's model the beginning of the declining phase has exogenous causes; among these Fanno underlines sudden variations of the propensity to save and or extraordinarily poor yields of important harvests. The last cause is discussed also by Tugan-Baranowski, whereas Aftalion asserts that the beginning of the downward path has endogenous causes; to be more precise it is due to incompatibilities arising among the dynamics of the different sectors[29].

As far as the author of the present paper knows these theories have never been mathematically formalized, apart of the simple but interesting model of Delli Gatti and Gallegati[30] and in some sense of Lorenz's contribution[31].

1.2 General outline of the model

The model we are going to develop in the present chapter aims to provide a formal analysis of overproduction crises qualitatively described by the above mentioned theories[32]. Moreover we want to exploit our model in order to discuss how different types of technical progress may modify their outbreaks and their evolution.

1.2.1 Specificity of each sector

Characterizing features of the model is to make specific assumptions for each sector. More precisely we take into account of how the specific char-

---

[25] See Tugan-Baranowski (1913).

[26] See Fanno (1931).

[27] See Hicks (1965) and (1974).

[28] See Aftalion (1913) see also Aftalion (1927).

[29] We refer to Hagemann and Landesmann (1996) for a stimulating and exhautive review of the tradition which dominated continental European business-cycle research from the late nineteenth century up to the Second World War.

[30] See Delli Gatti Gallegati (1991).

[31] See Lorenz (1987).

[32] A preliminary version of this model has been introduced in Gozzi and Nardini (2000).

acteristics of the goods produced by each sector influence the structure of the market where these goods are traded.

Hicks recognized the importance of this issue, but this idea has not been implemented in formal models and it is usual to assume that all markets have the same structure both in neo-classical and in Leontief or gravitational models.

1.2.2 Different forms of technical progress

We shall deal with different cases of technical progress, both in the consumption goods sector and in the capital goods one. Common features of all these cases are that technical progresses always are exogenous and disembodied.

On the one hand we consider cases of technical progress arising once and for all: they can not be systematically pursued by firms. On the other hand they display their effects on all existing productive capital; thus they are not embodied in the new capital goods to be produced after the diffusion of the innovation. In this sense they can be considered as the effects of a process of learning by doing: they consist in a new and more efficient use of already available technologies. We do not consider the introduction of a new technology which requires new types capital goods.

Since this type of technical progress is the consequence either of some scientific discovery or of some technical invention, it can not be foreseen and hence it is unexpected[33].

1.2.3 Multisector models and international economics

Our multisector approach can be easily generalized to treat cases of open economy. The foreign production my by described as taking place in some further sectors with their own structure and characteristics, taking carefully into account the interconnections among domestic and foreign sectors.

We are going to apply this strategy to describe the interplay between a large developed country and a small developing one

---

[33] As Faber and Proops correctly observe, forecasting a scientific discovery is equivalent to making it. See Faber and Proops (1990).

2 Assumptions of the Model

2.1 Common features of the two sectors

Before we pass to describe each sector and its specificities, we provide a short overview on the common features of both sectors.

Firms within each sector are alike and this will allow us to make use of the "representative" firm's concept. This assumption is required in order to keep at a minimum level the disaggregation of the model; in our model, in fact, firms are "price-makers".

2.1.1 The technology

We start describing the technology. We consider a Leontief-type fixed co-efficients production function with two complementary production factors: labor and fixed capital (see (3.1)). Any concrete unit of capital has a given output capacity and requires a given complement of labor[1], i.e. there is no substitutability between labor and capital.

The aim of this assumption is two fold. First we want to throw some light on possible bottlenecks in the growth path and in the capital accumulation process: a production function allowing for large substitutability

---

[1]"we have in mind 'the common causal-empirical belief that in the short run the scope for changing factor proportions is small" See Solow Tobin von Weizsaecker and Yaari (1966). We refer also to the citation of Lowe in subsection 1.1.4.

might somehow hide problems arising from scarcities of some production factors.

Second the fixed coefficients production function allows a very simple representation of any type of technical progress: for instance, an increase of the marginal productivity of labor in the consumption goods sector is simply represented by an decrease of the corresponding coefficient l_1 of the Leontief production function (3.1). Labor is perfectly elastic and the real wage rate is constant throughout the analysis. For instance we can assume that labor can be supplied by temporary immigration. However wage rigidity may be explained also by Phelps's shirking model[2]; according to it "the equilibrium wage that each firm will choose to pay can be determined independently of the firm's decision about how many workers to hire, how much to produce, or how to price its product"[3].

2.1.2 Profit and investment

Investment decisions of firms play a central role in the dynamic of a capitalist economy. Two factors have to be considered: allocation of capital to the firms by capitalists, and the actual use of the sum so determined by entrepreneurs, who can either decide to use only a part of it or to resort to the credit in order to achieve a higher level of investment.

As anticipated in section 1.1.3, we assume that in normal conditions the remuneration rate of fixed capital in both sectors are such that capitalists are indifferent at the sector where they invest. Therefore, under normal conditions, profits not spent on consumption are reinvested in the sector whence they originated[4] (see (3.2)). We describe in the following subsections 3.2 and 3.3 how firms in each sector modify their investment decisions when the economy moves away from equilibrium[5].

2.2 The consumption goods sector

2.2.1 Price decisions

"Typical end-products of manufacturing industry no longer consists of objectively standardizable goods, which can be treated on competitive whole-

---

[2] See Phelps (1995).

[3] See Woodford (1990).

[4] We may term this the self financing case. The crucial role of internal finance (retained earnings) in the expansion of a firm is discussed in Judd and Petersen (1986) section 3, where there is also an interesting list of references.

[5] The model covers the case of capitalists that are entrepreneurs in one of the two sectors or, more generally, capitalists and entrepreneurs in each sector belong to the same class; in this case the gross profit is distributed as remuneration and accumulated profit.

saler markets: they have become much more various, new products and new varieties being continually devised"[6] .

Moreover " since the product is specialized, no other manufacturer producing anything exactly like it, any merchant to whom he sells it directly must be dependent on him for supply. The merchant must thus be acting, in this part of his business, as manufacturer's agent. So we have an important example of vertical integration previously noticed: manufacturing and selling come in substance under the same control".

"There were two functions which we were attributing to our secondary merchants and their market: stockholding and price formation. As we saw they are nearly allied; so it is here. The selling department is able to set price and make it effective by holding stocks, so the price that is set can be chosen as a matter of policy"[7].

"Thus the diversified markets has a tendency to be what I have called a fix price market, meaning not that prices do not change, but that there is a force which makes for stabilization"[8].

More precisely, "it is not implied by the description Fixprice method that prices are never to change - only that they do not necessarily change whenever there is demand-supply disequilibrium"[9].

"If, when demand exceeds output, there are stocks that can be thrown in to fill the gap, it is not obvious that the price does not has to rise; a market in which stock changes substitute for price changes (at least up to a point) is readily intelligible"[10]

The aim of our model is to take into account all the facts described above: thus we assume that the firms in the consumption goods sector do not know the demand when they take their production decisions.

Hence they hold inventories[11] in order to cope with possible unexpected increases of the demand without resorting to too sudden and large increases of prices. On the other hand, if they want to avoid significant price falls[12], they must increase stocks when the scheduled production exceeds the demand (see (3.9)).

---

[6] See Hicks (1989), p. 23.

[7] See Hicks (1989), p. 24.

[8] See Hicks (1989), p. 25.

[9] See Hicks (1965), p. 78.

[10] See Hicks (1965), p. 79.

[11] This may be understood also in the sense that "retails stores functions as inventories mediating the flow of supplied and demaned commodities without the interventoin of a centralized coordination or a complicated and time consuming market bargaining and negotiation procedures...Ordering mechanisms with accompanying backlogs and variable delivery delays together with inventory fluctuations provide a flow of information that facilitates adjustment to equilibria in commodity supply and demand", Day (1984).

[12] Remember that, since the choice of the price is a matter of poilcy, the price become a relevant characteristic of the good and thus sudden wide changes should possibly be avoided.

Thus "we do have to use the concept of stock equilibrium: for it is by the absence of stock equilibrium that disequilibrium itself is carried forward"[13].

"To sum up, stocks and flows may be assigned a critical role in identifying linkages between different accounting periods. In particular, the relationship between equilibrium of stocks and equilibrium of flows makes events within the current period (flows) to influence the maintenance of stock equilibrium"[14].

We assume that the relevant variable that firms uses in order to detect stock disequilibrium is the ratio of inventories to the productive capacity; we call this ratio *inventory level* and denote it by s (see (3.7)).

We assume that firms in the consumption goods sector reacts to stock disequilibrium rising prices when the inventory level is below its target value and decreasing them in the opposite case (see (3.8)).

2.2.2. Decisions to produce

Also the decisions to produce are subject to the need of pursuing the stock equilibrium. Therefore we assume that, under normal conditions, firms have a margin of unused productive capacity; in such a way they can take advantage of unexpected and sudden favorable situations such as, for instance, shifts in the aggregate demand curve.

The immediate effect of such a shift is a decline of stocks, but as soon as firms realize that stock disequilibrium is increasing, they increase the productive capacity utilization rate. Conversely, when the inventory level is above its target value, firms reduce the utilization rate (see 3.16).

Thus the *productive capacity utilization rate u* (see (3.15)) will exceed its normal value when the inventory level is below its normal value and conversely. When stock are in equilibrium u will decrease when it is above its normal level and decrease in the opposite case.

"There is no need to assume that there is a single optimum output for which the plant is designed; it is better, being more realistic, to think of it as having a *regular* range of outputs which is reasonably well fitted to produce"[15].

We assume that firms in this sector always maintain either enough stocks or sufficient productive capacity to satisfy the demand: in the consumption goods market rationing never occurs.

---

[13]See Hicks (1965), p. 80.

[14]It is clear that the flow disequilibrium may be corrected within each accounting period, whereas the correction of stock disequilibrium generally takes several accounting periods. See Scazzieri (1992), p. 228.

[15]See Hicks (1989), p. 22.

2.2.3 Decisions to invest

Coming to investment decisions in the consumption goods sector, since we are assuming that workers have no propensity for saving, in our model total savings equal the accumulated profit, i.e. the part of the profit not spent on the consumption goods market.

When equilibrium prevails, the economy develops along a steady state growth path (see chapter 4) with constant growth and profit rates. Hence the assumption that investment in each sector equals the accumulated profit is perfectly acceptable.

On the other hand, when the economy deviates from this path, the rates of growth and profit may widely oscillate in both sectors and investment becomes risky[16]. Since investment in capital goods is assumed to be totally irreversible (see section 2.3) "the investment decision is simply the decision to pay the sunk cost and in return to get an asset whose value can fluctuate"; the asset "is simply the expected present value of the stream of profits (or losses) it would generate"[17].

In this case actual investment takes place when the firms exercise their "option to invest"[18] and the optimal strategy may be either to wait or to anticipate investment, according to the expectations on returns[19]

Thus we assume that the normal investment (3.2) is "corrected" by taking into account market disequilibrium. This amounts to say that investment is determined by a non linear accelerator: When the productive capacity utilization rate is above its target value firms invest more than the normal amount (3.2), since the profit rate is above its equilibrium value (see (19.3) and (19.4)). Symmetrically, when the productive capacity utilization rate is below its target value, firms invest less than in equilibrium[20] (see (3.18) and (3.19)).

On the other hand, since firms in the capital goods sector do not hold inventories, there is no mean to prevent the demand to temporary exceed the supply, when this happens rationing begins (see (3.29)); thus investment is subject to the constraint of productive capacity of the capital goods sector.

---

[16] This is to be undersood not in the sense that the outcome of a present decision depends on the realization of some random variable, but in the sense that agents'forecasts are likely to involve sizable mistakes outside the seady state growth path, since perfect forsight is likely to obtain only when the traders environment is repetitive enough.

[17] See Dixit and Pindyck (1994) p. 13.

[18] See Dixit and Pindyck (1994) chapter 5.

[19] We observe that in our model investment expenditures have both the characteristics required by Dixit Pindyck (1994) p. 137: "First the expenditures are at least partly irreversible...Second these investment may be delayed".

[20] The assumption that fixed productive capital is specific to the sector prevents capitalists to move it from a sector to the other even when the former looses its profitability. In this event the surplus condition (3.5) guarantees that going on producing diminishes losses.

2.3 The capital goods sector

2.3.1 Decisions to produce

Not only consumption goods, but also capital goods are highly specialized products in the modern industrial economy. They are generally either specifically designed or at least deeply adapted for the specific productive plan where they are going to be utilized.

Therefore we assume that the firms in the capital goods sector produce to order. "This fact often happens, ...industries which produce costly or quite special machines construct these machines on orders given to them beforehand by the producers"[21] . Thus they know the demand in advance and are able to produce exactly the demanded amount, provided that the demand does not exceeds the productive capacity of the sector. In this case the demand D_2 for capital goods undergoes rationing and the demand coming from firms in the capital goods sector itself is satisfied first (see (3.24), (3.28), and (3.29)).

2.3.2 Price decisions

In the case of rationing, firms in the capital goods sector react to disequilibrium increasing the price p_2 of capital goods; the larger is the disequilibrium, the faster is the increase (see (3.30)).

We remark explicitly that price and production decisions in both sectors described above are plausible in the sense that they make only modest information processing demands on agents.

Coherently with our assumptions on their nature, we assume that, once installed in a firm in one of the two sectors, capital goods become specific and can not be moved to the other sector[22]. Neither can the specialized equipment intended for use in the capital goods sector be transferred to the consumption goods sector, nor can equipment suitable for production in the first sector be transferred to the second sector[23]. Thus we do not need to consider prices of used capital goods.

---

[21]This observation goes back to Bresciani-Turroni (1936) p. 165.

[22]"A new machine will be sold to any factory that demands it, while a machine that has already been set up in a factory will not usually be transferred to another facotory even if the factory that owns the machine is overequipped and some other factory is underequipped...Machines placed in different sectors are different goods and have different spheres of transference" (see Morishima (1969)). A fundamental contribution in this direction is the well known paper of Bliss (1968).

[23]See Lowe (1976) p. 292.

2.3.3 Decisions to invest

Coming to the decisions to invest of firms in the capital goods sector, we assume that in this sector actual investment always equals normal investment. We explicitly remark that there is no need of a second accelerator; since there are two only sectors in the model, the accelerator in the consumption goods sector acts as a decelerator in the capital goods one (see (3.32)). On the other hand rationing accelerates investment in the capital goods sector at the expenses of the consumption goods one.

The mechanism of allocation of capital described so far (subsections 2.3.1, 2.3.2, 2.3.3) needs perhaps some final clarifying comments. The mobility of capital between different sectors results from three distinct behavioral assumptions.

1. A (positive) excess demand of one of the two goods boosts its price: this rises the profitability of the corresponding sector and lowers the profitability of the other one, so that more and more profits can be reinvested in the former sector, thus subtracting investment to the latter. Moreover, if the other sector is forced to reduce its remuneration of capital, then it is prevented to obtain new investment too. Obviously excess supply has completely reverse effects on profitability and investment.

2. When the level of inventories of consumption goods are lowered by a demand exceeding the productive capacity, the accelerator forces the investment in this sector to exceed the profit made within the sector, rising the share of the consumption goods sector in total investment. The reverse is true when a weak demand for consumption goods blows up inventories.

3. Rationing of capital goods, caused by an excess demand, compresses the investment in the consumption goods sector, thus moving capital from it to the capital goods sector. On the other hand remuneration differentials between the sectors drive investment towards the sector ensuring the higher remuneration rate.

The preceding analysis shows that the mobility of capital is guaranteed; however its ultimate cause is not profitability differentials, but differentials of either the remuneration rates or (expected) growth rate of the outputs of both sectors. Even if agents are not well informed of firms (and thus are unable continuously to detect profitability differentials), they can obviously observe the current remuneration of capital and may easily forecast a high rate of growth of a sector together with its profitability, as they observe an excess demand in the market of the corresponding good and the related price rise[24].

Also in this case we have chosen a set of assumptions making limited demands on agents' information processing. We do not dwell into the question whether capitalists or salaried managers are profit maximizers or growth rate maximizers. It is clear that growth independent of profitability levels can not be their ultimate objective. On the other hand an expected growth of the sector may be a better signal than simply the present profit rate[25].

Last but not least we underline the complexity of this link between investment, profitability, and growth rates.

We conclude this section stressing that the model does not deal explicitly with monetary problems and financial markets: the nominal money supply is assumed to match the nominal money demand at every time.

In this part we do not introduce the government in the model; we are going to discuss its role and the impact of different fiscal policies on the dynamic of this model in the third part.

---

[24] We think that this is in line with Hicks' opinion "I have actually seen business decisions being made on the basis of projected balance sheets. I think that is the rational way to make business decisions. A lot of mathematical models, including some of my own, are really terribly much in the air.". Cited after Klamer and Mc Closkey (1992).

[25] In the sense of Dixit and Pindyk (1994), see subsection 2.2.3 again.

3 The Equations of the Model

This chapter is devoted to the formalization of the assumptions presented in the preceding one. The first section describes the common features of both sectors, the second one deals with the consumption goods sector and the third one with the capital goods sector.

3.1 Common features of both sectors

3.1.1 Input and output

If Y_i denotes the output of the i-th sector, K_i and L_i the input of capital and labor respectively, the output of the i-th sector is given by the Leontief-type production function

$$Y_i = \min\left\{b_i K_i, \frac{b_i}{l_i} L_i\right\}.$$ (3.1)

Obviously b_i and $\frac{b_i}{l_i}$ are the marginal productivities of capital and labor in the i-th sector, respectively.

3.1.2 Profit and investment

The level of investment that firms in the i-th sector may attain by using the purchasing power obtained from capitalists is

$$I_i^n = \max\left\{\delta K_i + \frac{\Pi_i^a}{k_i}, 0\right\},$$ (3.2)

here K_i denotes the stock of fixed capital in the i-th sector, δ the depreciation rate (the same in both sectors), Π_i^a is the accumulated profit (see also
(3.10) and (3.11)), and k_i the money capital necessary to realize a unitary
(fixed) investment in the i-th sector. Thus in equilibrium the actual investment I_i of firms in the i-th sector equals the normal[1] one I_i^n. In any case
the evolution of the stock of fixed capital engaged in production in the i-th
sector is

$$\dot{K}_i = I_i - \delta K_i. \tag{3.3}$$

3.2   The consumption goods sector

3.2.1   Prices and wages

If w denotes the real wage rate and p_1 the unitary price of the consumption
good, the income of workers employed in the consumption goods sector W_1
is

$$W_1 = w p_1 L_1 = w p_1 \frac{l_1}{b_1} Y_1. \tag{3.4}$$

We assume no saving out of wages; therefore the whole income (3.4) will
be spent on the consumption goods market.

The production can obviously take place only if the condition

$$Y_1 p_1 - W_1 > 0 \tag{3.5}$$

holds; taking into account (3.1) and (3.4) this may be rewritten in the
following form

$$b_1 - w l_1 > 0. \tag{3.6}$$

Inequality (3.6) means that the real wage rate w is compatible with the
productive technology employed in the first sector, we obviously assume
that this condition holds. We stress that condition (3.6) has to be regarded
as a surplus condition, not as a profit condition.

If S_1 denotes the stock (measured in physical units) accumulated by firms
in the first sector, the inventory level is

$$s = S_1 / b_1 K_1 \tag{3.7}$$

If firms in this sector consider $\bar{s}$ the *normal level of inventories*, we assume
that they adjust the price p_1 of consumption goods in order to keep the
actual level s near to its target[2] level $\bar{s}$. Therefore price decisions of firms

---

[1] For a discussion of this concept we refer to Hicks (1974).

[2] It is outside the scope of this book to discuss how this target is chosen.. We refer to
Arrow Karling and Scarf (1958) and to Holt Modigliani Muth and Simon (1960) for a
thorough discussion of the complex interplay of production, inventories, and prices.

may be formalized in the following way

$$\dot{p}_1 = p_1 g_1(s), \tag{3.8}$$

where $g_1 \in C^{(1)}$ is a function such that $g_1(\bar{s}) = 0$, $dg_1/ds = g_1' < 0$ and with $\lim_{s \to +\infty} g_1(s) = -\infty$ and $\lim_{s \to 0^+} sg_1(s) = +\infty^3$.

Remark 1 *It is easy to take account of the upward flexibility and downward stickiness of prices assuming that function $g(s)$ is steeper (even much steeper) as $s > 0$.*

3.2.2 Profit and production

The evolution of inventories S_1 in the consumption goods sector depends on the gap between total output Y_1 and demand for consumption goods D_1; formally this means

$$\dot{S}_1 = Y_1 - D_1. \tag{3.9}$$

The net profit generated by the first sector Π_1 is the difference between the value of the total output and the aggregate wage bill, paid to the workers, plus the amortisation of the depreciated fixed capital

$$\Pi_1 = Y_1 p_1 - (W_1 + \delta K_1 p_2), \tag{3.10}$$

where p_2 is the unitary price of the capital good (measured in physical units). The amount of profit is divided into two parts, one for consumption Π_1^c and the other for accumulation Π_1^a hence

$$\Pi_1 = \Pi_1^c + \Pi_1^a \tag{3.11}$$

We assume that the distributed part of profit is proportional to the stock of productive fixed capital employed in the sector

$$\Pi_1^c = d_1 K_1 p_2, \tag{3.12}$$

here d_1 is the dividend.

Remark 2 *We stress the point that accumulated profits, Π_1^a, need not be positive. In this case firms in the sector are not only unable to make (positive) net investment but also to replace depreciated fixed capital. Moreover, the surplus condition (3.6) does not guarantees enough output to pay the scheduled remuneration (3.12) of the fixed capital.*

---

[3]This condition means that firms eventually decide strong price increases to prevent exhaustion of resources.

When this happens this remuneration in paid resorting to the inventories, whenever they are sufficient[4].

If we denote the aggregate wage bill and the distributed part of profit of the capital goods sector by W_2 e Π_2^a respectively, the demand of consumption goods D_1 is given by

$$D_1 = \frac{\Pi_1^c + \Pi_2^c + W_1 + W_2}{p_1}. \qquad (3.13)$$

The total capital C_1 engaged in the production of consumption goods is the sum of the value of fixed productive capital plus the value of inventories

$$C_1 = K_1 p_2 + S_1 p_1 \qquad (3.14)$$

If we denote by u the productive capacity utilization rate

$$u = Y_1/b_1 K_1 \qquad (3.15)$$

and by $\bar{u}$ its *normal value* $(0 < \bar{u} < 1)^5$, a possible formalization of firms' decisions to produce may be the following

$$\dot{u} = F(u, s), \qquad (3.16)$$

where $F \in C^1$ is a function such that $F(\bar{u}, \bar{s}) = 0$, $\partial F/\partial u < 0$, $\partial F/\partial s < 0$ and with $\lim_{u \to 0^+} F(u, s) = +\infty$ and $\lim_{u \to 1^-} F(u, s) = -\infty$ for any $s > 0$. Thus decisions to produce reacts to both stock disequilibrium $(s \neq \bar{s})$ and disequilibrium in production $(u \neq \bar{u})$.

The conditions on g_1 and F ensure that the production and price decisions in the consumption goods sector prevent the exhaustion of the inventories and, therefore, rationing does not occur in this sector; as a result, when $i = 1$, formula (3.1) simplifies to

$$Y_1 = \frac{b_1}{l_1} L_1.$$

3.2.3 *Investment*

We remember that u and s denote the capacity utilization rate and the inventory level respectively (see (3.15) and (3.7)), moreover we define unitary capital engaged in the production of the consumption goods the rate (see (3.2))

---

[4] The assumption that fixed productive capital is specific to the sector prevents capitalists to move it from a sector to the other even when the former looses its profitability. In this event the surplus condition (3.5) guarantees that going on producing diminishes losses.

[5] We do not attempt to enter the problem of the evaluatoin of $\bar{u}$; obviuosly $\bar{u} \gg 0$ and for instance a first rough lower bound may be $\bar{u} > 0.8$. We again refer to Holt Modigliani Muth and Simon (1960) (see subsection 3.2.1). In the same way we do not dwell on how firms determine the normal level $\bar{s}$ of the inventories.

$$k = k_1 = \frac{C_1}{K_1} \qquad (3.17)$$

where C_1 is the total capital engaged in production in the first sector (3.14).

As we have supposed, the desired gross investment of the entrepreneurs of the first sector I_1^a equals the accumulated profit in normal conditions, is accelerated as the capacity utilization rate u exceeds its normal value $\bar{u}$ and decelerated in the opposite situation (see subsection 1.1.3). "It is perhaps very difficult to trace the steps by which change [capital mobility] is effected: it is probably effected by a manufacturer not absolutely changing his employment, but only lessening the quantity of capital he has in his employment"[6]. Here formally

$$I_1^a = \max\left\{\left(\delta K_1 + \frac{\Pi_1^a}{k}\right) h(u), 0\right\} = I_1^n h(u) \qquad (3.18)$$

where h is an increasing $C^{(1)}$ function such that

$$h(u) \begin{cases} > 1 & \text{if} \quad u > \bar{u} \\ < 1 & \text{if} \quad u < \bar{u} \end{cases}, \qquad (3.19)$$
$$\lim_{u \to 1-} h(u) = +\infty .$$

Hence I_1^a is the ex ante gross investment in the first sector; ex post investment I_1 may be less than I_1^a, since the supply of capital goods may be insufficient to cope with the demand[7] (see (3.29) and (3.24)).

3.3   The capital goods sector

3.3.1   Wages and profits

Also the relations connecting total output Y_2, employment L_2, aggregate wage bill W_2, profit Π_2 of the capital goods sector are analogous to the corresponding ones in the consumption goods sector

$$W_2 = wL_2 p_1, \qquad (3.20)$$

$$\Pi_2 = Y_2 p_2 - (W_2 + \delta K_2 p_2), \qquad (3.21)$$

---

[6] See Ricardo (1817) ch. 4 p. 48. It is clear that the same is true in the opposite direction.

[7] The max formulation is consistent with the assumption of non transerability of used capital goods from one sector to the other.

$$\Pi_2^c = d_2 K_2 p_2; \tag{3.22}$$

Since we are assuming no saving out of wages, the whole income (3.20) will be spent on the consumption goods market.

With the same notation as before Π_2^c and Π_2^a denote distributed and accumulated profit respectively in the capital goods sector (compare (3.21) and (3.22) with (3.10) and (3.11) respectively); hence we have (see (3.12))

$$\Pi_2 = \Pi_2^a + \Pi_2^c \tag{3.23}$$

3.3.2 Output and demand

The decisions to produce of this sector may be formalized in the following way

$$Y_2 = \begin{cases} D_2 & \text{if} \quad D_2 \leq b_2 K_2 \\ b_2 K_2 & \text{if} \quad D_2 > b_2 K_2 \end{cases}, \tag{3.24}$$

where D_2 is the demand of capital goods (see (3.27)).

Also in this case (see (3.5)) we assume that the production of capital goods take place only if the surplus condition

$$Y_2 p_2 - W_2 > 0 \tag{3.25}$$

holds; in this case, however, the meaning of (3.25) is different from that of (3.5), since it entails an upper bound for the relative price $\frac{p_1}{p_2}$ of the consumption good in terms of capital good; precisely

$$\frac{p_1}{p_2} \leq \frac{b_2}{wl_2} \tag{3.26}$$

We can interpret this condition as an upper bound for the nominal wage rate wp_1 which guarantees its compatibility with the technical production conditions (3.1) and the price of the capital good p_2.

As we are supposing that firms in the capital goods sector produce to order, they have no reason for holding inventories, hence $S_2 = 0$ and the supply of capital goods always coincides with the total output Y_2; it coincides also with the demand

$$D_2 = I_1^a + I_2 \tag{3.27}$$

when the demand does not exceeds the productive capacity of the sector; in formula (3.27) I_2 denotes the gross investment of firms in the second sector. Formally

$$Y_2 = D_2 \quad \text{if} \quad D_2 \leqslant b_2 K_2 \; . \tag{3.28}$$

In the opposite case, $D_2 > b_2 K_2$, rationing of the capital goods supply can not be avoided. In this case we suppose that the demand I_2 due to the capital goods sector is entirely satisfied, while the demand coming from the consumption goods sector is destined to remain partly unsatisfied. So the ex post investment in the first sector is given by

$$I_1 = Y_2 - I_2 \qquad (3.29)$$

3.3.3 Price and investment

Formally price decision of firms in the capital goods sector may be given the form[8]

$$\dot{p}_2 = p_2 g_2 \left(\frac{D_2 - Y_2}{Y_2} \right), \qquad (3.30)$$

where $g_2 \in C^1$ is a function that satisfies $g_2(0) = 0$, $g_2' > 0$ and $\lim_{s \to +\infty} g_2(s) = +\infty$.

Since it is impossible to use inventories to in order to pay dividends, the distributed profit in the capital goods sector can not exceed the surplus of this sector

$$\Pi_2^c = \min\{d_2 K_2 p_2, Y_2 p_2 - W_2\} \qquad (3.31)$$

In the capital goods sector the money capital necessary to realize a unitary investment[9] is $k_2 = p_2$; hence (3.2) becomes

$$I_2 = \max\left\{ \delta K_2 + \frac{\Pi_2^a}{p_2}, 0 \right\} = I_2^n \qquad (3.32)$$

---

[8] We explicitly notice that the normalization introduced in (3.30) is the same we have used in (3.7), (3.8) and (3.15), (3.16).

This can be easily seen having in mind that, if $D_2 - Y_2 > 0$, then $Y_2 = b_2 K_2$ (see (3.24)) and hence $\frac{D_2 - Y_2}{Y_2} = \frac{D_2 - Y_2}{b_2 K_2}$.

[9] Remember that the capital good sector doesn't accumulate inventories.

4 The Dynamical System

This chapter is devoted to the description of the evolution of the most relevant economic variables in the different regimes in which the economy described by our model may operate.

4.1 Relative variables and profitability conditions

4.1.1 Output, investment, and profit in terms of relative variables

Since the general price level and the fixed capital stocks in both sectors depend only on the initial conditions, it is possible to express all relations introduced in (3.2) and (3.3) simply by means of the stock of fixed capital in the first sector, the capacity utilization rate (3.15), the inventory level (3.7), the relative price p of consumption goods in term of capital goods

$$p = \frac{p_1}{p_2} \tag{4.1}$$

and the relative capitalization z of the second sector with respect to the first one

$$z = \frac{K_2}{K_1} \tag{4.2}$$

In particular we can normalize the prices so that we have $p_1 = p$ and $p_2 = 1$.

We begin considering the first sector; from formulas (3.4) (3.17) and (3.10) we obtain respectively

$$W_1 = wl_1 puK_1, \tag{4.3}$$

$$\Pi_1 = \left(\left(1 - \frac{wl_1}{b_1} \right) pb_1 u - \delta \right) K_1, \tag{4.4}$$

and

$$k = 1 + b_1 sp; \tag{4.5}$$

then we set

$$\beta = \frac{1}{k} \left(1 - \frac{wl_1}{b_1} \right) p, \tag{4.6}$$

$$\alpha = \delta - \frac{d_1 + \delta}{k} \tag{4.7}$$

and substitute (4.4), (4.6), and (4.7) into (3.18); taking into account (3.11) and (3.12) we obtain

$$I_1^a = \max \left\{ (\alpha + b_1 \beta u) \, h \, (u) \, K_1, 0 \right\}. \tag{4.8}$$

Finally, if we denote the growth rate of the fixed capital stock K_1 of the consumption goods sector by ρ, from (3.3) and (4.8) we obtain

$$\dot{K}_1 = \rho K_1 \tag{4.9}$$

with

$$\rho = (\alpha + b_1 \beta u) \, h \, (u) - \delta \tag{4.10}$$

As far as the capital goods sector is concerned, if the productive capacity is sufficient and no rationing occurs (see (3.28)) and if dividends can be regularly paid (see (3.31)), we have

$$\Pi_2 = \left(1 - \frac{wl_2}{b_2} p \right) Y_2 - \delta K_2 \tag{4.11}$$

$$\Pi_2^a = \left(1 - \frac{wl_2}{b_2} p \right) Y_2 - (d_2 + \delta) K_2 \tag{4.12}$$

$$I_2 = \max \left\{ \left(1 - \frac{wl_2}{b_2} p \right) Y_2 - d_2 K_2, 0 \right\} \tag{4.13}$$

On the other hand, from (3.27), (3.28), and (4.13) we obtain

$$Y_2 = \left(1 - \frac{wl_2}{b_2} p \right) Y_2 + (I_1 - dK_2) \tag{4.14}$$

whence we can get Y_2 in terms of I_1 and K_2, having in mind that total output can obviously never become negative

$$Y_2 = \max \left\{ \frac{b_2}{wl_2 p} \left(I_1 - dK_2 \right), 0 \right\} \tag{4.15}$$

Since we are assuming that rationing does not occur, ex ante and ex post investment coincide $I_1^a = I_1$; thus, if we introduce (4.8) into (4.15), we obtain

$$Y_2 = \frac{b_2}{wl_2 p} \left[\left(\alpha + b_1 \beta u \right) h \left(u \right) - d_2 z \right] K_1 \tag{4.16}$$

whence, having in mind (3.20), we obtain

$$W_2 = \left[\left(\alpha + b_1 \beta u \right) h \left(u \right) - d_2 z \right] K_1. \tag{4.17}$$

4.1.2   Profitability conditions

We have already stressed that formulas (4.16) e (4.17) holds under the condition $I_1 > d_2 K_2$; this condition is satisfied if and only if

$$z < \frac{\alpha + b_1 \beta u}{d_2} h \left(u \right). \tag{4.18}$$

Inequality (4.18) can be rephrased using the relative price (4.1) and takes the following form

$$p > \frac{d_1 h(u) + d_2 z}{\left(\left(b_1 - wl_1 \right) u + \delta b_1 s \right) h(u) - d_2 b_1 s z} \tag{4.19}$$

In order that $Y_2 > 0$, it is obviously necessary that $I_1 > 0$ (see (4.15)); and this is true if and only if

$$p > \frac{d_2}{\left(b_1 - wl_1 \right) u + \delta b_1 s} \tag{4.20}$$

Firms in the capital goods sector are able to distribute profits in the scheduled measure (3.12) if and only if $I_2 > 0$; this happens if the condition

$$z < \left(1 - \frac{wl_2}{b_2} p \right) \frac{\alpha + b_1 \beta u}{d_2} h \left(u \right) \tag{4.21}$$

holds. Inequality (4.21) obviously implies (4.18) and this in turn implies (4.20) via (4.19)[1].

---

[1] This means that in the present model the capital goods sector is more likely to loose its profitability than the consumption goods one. In this sense investment in former sector is riskier than in last one; this justifies the assumption that the remuneration rate is not the same in both sectors. In order to make investment indifferent to the sector it is necessary the $d_2 > d_1$.

4.1.3 Rationing

We conclude observing that rationing in the capital goods market does not occur if and only if the relative capitalization satisfies the lower bound

$$z \geq \frac{\alpha + b_1 \beta u}{w l_2 p + d_2} h(u) \tag{4.22}$$

Hence, in order that both (4.21) and (4.22) may be met together, it is necessary and sufficient that

$$p \leq \frac{b_2 - d_2}{w l_2} \tag{4.23}$$

Inequality (4.23) can be interpreted as an upper bound on the nominal wage rate pw, just like the condition (3.26); it is evident that condition (4.23) implies (3.26).

4.2 The dynamical system under normal conditions

Now we are able to write the evolution equations for the economic system when both sectors generate enough profit to guarantee the scheduled remuneration of fixed capital and capital goods are not rationed; we call these conditions normal state of the economy.

4.2.1 Evolution of the inventory level

As shown in section 4.1, the economy develops in normal conditions means that (4.20), (4.21), (4.22), and (4.23) hold.

We have already introduced equations for the evolution (3.16) of the capacity utilization rate u and the evolutions (3.8) (3.30) of the prices p_1, p_2 . Now we want to write an equation for the evolution of the inventory level s in terms of u , p_1 and p_2 . Combining equations (3.9) and (3.3), we obtain

$$\dot{s} = \frac{Y_1 - D_1}{b_1 K_1} - s \frac{I_1 - \delta K_1}{K_1} \tag{4.24}$$

then, using (3.13), (3.12), (3.31), (4.3), (4.17) and (4.8), from (2.54) we obtain the desired equation

$$\dot{s} = \frac{k}{b_1 p} (\alpha + b_1 \beta u)(1 - h(u)) \tag{4.25}$$

4.2.2 Evolution of the relative capitalization

From equation (3.3) it is easy to obtain an equation for the evolution of the relative capitalization (4.2); this can be done first introducing (4.13) and (4.16) into (3.3) with $i = 2$

$$\dot{K_2} = \frac{b_2 - wl_2p}{wl_2p} \left(\alpha + b_1\beta u \right) h(u) K_1 - \left(\delta + d_2 \frac{b_2}{wl_2p} \right) K_2 \qquad (4.26)$$

Then, using formula (4.9), we quickly obtain

$$\dot{z} = \left(\left(\alpha + b_1\beta u \right) h(u) + d_2 \frac{b_2}{wl_2p} \right) z + \frac{b_2 - wl_2p}{wl_2p} \left(\alpha + b_1\beta u \right) h(u) \qquad (4.27)$$

4.2.3 Evolution of the relative price

We conclude this section obtaining an equation for the evolution of the relative price (4.1) from equations (3.8) and (3.30)

$$\dot{p} = \left(g_1(s) - g_2 \left(\frac{d_2 + wl_2p - \left(\alpha + b_1\beta u \right) h(u)\frac{1}{z}}{b_2} \right) \right) \qquad (4.28)$$

The second term of the right hand side of equation (4.28) is obviously zero in the case, we are now examining, that there is no rationing of the capital goods (see condition (4.22)).

4.2.4 The differential system

So far we have obtained a 4×4 system of first order non linear differential equations in the unknown functions u , s , p , and z

$$\begin{cases} \dot{u} = F(u, s) \\ \dot{s} = \dfrac{k}{b_1 p} \left(\alpha + b_1\beta u \right) \left(1 - h(u) \right) \\ \dot{p} = g_1(s)\, p \\ \dot{z} = - \left(\left(\alpha + b_1\beta u \right) h(u) + d_2 \dfrac{b_2}{wl_2p} \right) z + \dfrac{b_2 - wl_2p}{wl_2p} \left(\alpha + b_1\beta u \right) h(u) \end{cases} \qquad (4.29)$$

In order to simplify notations, we put

$$G(u, s, p) = \frac{k}{b_1 p} \left(\alpha + b_1\beta u \right) \left(1 - h(u) \right) \qquad (4.30)$$

and

$$H(u, s, p, z) = - \left(\left(\alpha + b_1\beta u \right) h(u) + d_2 \frac{b_2}{wl_2p} \right) z + \frac{b_2 - wl_2p}{wl_2p} \left(\alpha + b_1\beta u \right) h(u) \qquad (4.31)$$

System (4.29) and equations (4.9), (4.10) fully describe the evolution of the economy under normal conditions.

4.3 Dynamical system when profits fall

As we have observed in subsection 4.1.2, a fall of profitability hits first and foremost the capital goods sector. In this subsection we treat the case when the capital goods sector does no longer generate enough profit to ensure the scheduled remuneration of fixed capital, while the consumption goods sector is still sufficiently profitable.

Formally this means that (4.21) does not hold, while (4.20) still holds.

4.3.1   Output and profits in the capital goods sector

Then from (3.28), (3.27), and (4.8) we can determine the total output of capital goods

$$Y_2 = (\alpha + b_1\beta u)\, h\,(u)\, K_1. \tag{4.32}$$

From (3.31) we deduce that the distributed profits of the capital goods sector under these assumptions are reduced to

$$\Pi_2^c = Y_2 - wpl_2 = \left(1 - \frac{wl_2}{b_2}p\right)(\alpha + b_1\beta u)\, h\,(u)\, K_1, \tag{4.33}$$

while from (3.15) and (4.32) it is possible to determine the aggregate wage bill payed to the workers in the capital goods sector

$$\frac{W_2}{p} = \frac{wl_2}{b_2}(\alpha + b_1\beta u)\, h\,(u)\, K_1. \tag{4.34}$$

4.3.2   Demand for consumption goods and evolution of the relative capitalization

Since the condition, under which the consumption goods sector operates, remain unchanged , we can easily calculate the demand of consumption goods from (3.13), (4.3), (4.4), (4.33), and (4.34) obtaining

$$D_1 = \frac{d_1}{p}K_1 + \frac{1}{p}\left(1 - \frac{wl_2}{b_2}p\right)(\alpha + b_1\beta u)\, h\,(u)\, K_1 + \tag{4.35}$$

$$\frac{wl_1}{b_1}b_1 u K_1 + \frac{wl_2}{b_2}(\alpha + b_1\beta u)\, h\,(u)\, K_1$$

By the same considerations exploited in section 2.4, it is easy to realize that the evolution equation for the inventory level (4.24) holds also under the present assumptions .

On the other hand the evolution equation for the relative capitalization is different, since from (4.33), (3.22), and (3.21) it is easy to see that we have $\Pi_2^a = -\delta K_2$: the fall of the profitability of the capital goods sector prevent firms even to replace the depreciated fixed capital. The differential equation for the relative capitalization, which replaces (4.31), is

$$\dot{z} = -(\alpha + b_1\beta u)\, h(u)z \tag{4.36}$$

4.3.3   The differential system

Thus we have found a new dynamical system; namely

$$
\begin{cases}
\dot{u} = F\left(u, s\right) \\
\dot{s} = \dfrac{k}{b_1 p} \left(\alpha + b_1 \beta u\right) \left(1 - h(u)\right) \\
\dot{p} = g_1\left(s\right) p \\
\dot{z} = -\left(\alpha + b_1 \beta u\right) h(u) z
\end{cases}
\tag{4.37}
$$

We call the differential system (4.37) the differential system of falling profits.

4.4   The dynamical system during the slump

A further decline of profitability eventually undermines also the remuneration rate of productive capital invested in the consumption goods sector; in this case investment in that sector is no longer convenient.

Formally this means that (4.20) does not hold.

Here we examine the case when the level of inventories of consumption goods is high enough to allow the payment of dividends out of them.

4.4.1   Evolution of the inventory level and the relative capitalization

To write down the new differential equations, we begin noticing that, if $I_1 = I_2 = 0$, then we obtain

$$
\dot{z} = 0
\tag{4.38}
$$

from (3.10), (3.3), and (4.13).

Since the total output of capital goods is zero, aggregate wage bill and distributed profits of this sector are obviously zero too $W_2 = 0$ and $\Pi_2^c = 0$, while the analogous quantities relative to the consumption goods sector W_1 and Π_1^c are still given by (3.15), (4.3), and (3.12) respectively; so the variations of the inventory level is given by

$$
\dot{s} = \frac{Y_1 - D_1}{b_1 K_1} - s \frac{\dot{K_1}}{K_1} = \left(1 - \frac{w l_1}{b_1}\right) u - \frac{d}{p b_1} + \delta s.
\tag{4.39}
$$

4.4.2 The differential system

Thus system (4.37) is now replaced with

$$
\begin{cases}
\dot{u} = F(u, s) \\
\dot{s} = \left(1 - \dfrac{wl_1}{b_1}\right) u - \dfrac{d}{pb_1} + \delta s \\
\dot{p} = g_1(s)\, p \\
\dot{z} = 0
\end{cases}
\tag{4.40}
$$

We call the differential system (4.40) the differential system of the slump.

4.5 The dynamical system when profit rates are far from equilibrium

If a strong demand for consumption goods let their price p_1 grow faster than the price p_2 of capital goods, profit in the consumption goods sector grows more and more, while it declines in the capital goods sector.

Thus it may happen that the production of capital goods is insufficient to satisfy the demand generated by the consumption goods sector on the one side and, on the other side, that investment in the capital goods sector is not yet convenient.

Obviously this situation is temporary and it can not last but for a relatively short time, but it occurs when the relative price p is such that neither (4.18) nor (4.22) hold, but (4.20) does.

4.5.1 Investment, output, and profit

In this case *ex post* investment I_1 in the consumption goods sector equals the maximum productive capacity of the capital goods sector precisely, since in this sector no investment is taking place. Hence we have

$$
\begin{aligned}
I_1 &= b_2 K_2 \\
\dot{K}_1 &= -\delta K_1 + b_2 K_2
\end{aligned}
\tag{4.41}
$$

while

$$
\begin{aligned}
I_2 &= 0 \\
\dot{K}_2 &= -\delta K_2
\end{aligned}
\tag{4.42}
$$

As far as total output, employment, and distributed profits in the consumption goods sector are concerned, formulas (3.15), (3.1), (3.4) and (3.12) still hold, while in the capital goods sector we now have the following relations

$$
Y_2 = b_2 K_2
\tag{4.43}
$$

$$L_2 = l_2 K_2 \tag{4.44}$$

$$W_2 = wl_2 p K_2 \tag{4.45}$$

$$\Pi_2^c = \left(1 - \frac{wl_2}{b_2}p\right) b_2 K_2. \tag{4.46}$$

The meaning of formulas (4.43) (4.25) and is clear: according to the former the capital good sector has reached its maximum capacity utilization rate while the second yields the employment necessary to maintain this level of output; the aggregate wage bill (4.26) is determined by (4.44) and (3.20) while distributed profits Π_2^c are given by (3.31).

4.5.2 Evolution of the inventory level

In order to calculate the variation of the inventory level in the present case, we begin determining the demand of consumption goods using (3.25), (3.12), (4.45), (4.46), and (3.13)

$$D_1 = \frac{d_1 K_1}{p} + \frac{\left(1 - \frac{wl_2}{b_2}p\right) b_2 K_2}{p} + wl_1 u K_1 + wl_2 K_2 \tag{4.47}$$

Then, having in mind (4.24), (4.43), (4.47), and (4.41), we obtain the evolution equation for the inventory level in the form

$$\dot{s} = \left(1 - \frac{wl_1}{b_1}\right) u - \frac{d_1}{b_1 p} - \frac{b_2}{b_1 p} z - s\left(b_2 z - \delta\right) \tag{4.48}$$

The evolution equation for the relative price p now is (4.1) where obviously $g_2 > 0$, while the evolution of the relative capitalization; z can be easily deduced from formulas (4.9), (4.41), and (4.42).

4.5.3 The differential system

Now the differential system describing the evolution of the economy becomes

$$\begin{cases} \dot{u} = F\left(u, s\right) \\ \dot{s} = \left(1 - \frac{wl_1}{b_1}\right) u - \frac{d_1}{b_1 p} - \frac{b_2}{b_1 p} z - s\left(b_2 z - \delta\right) \\ \dot{p} = \left(g_1\left(s\right) - g_2\left(\frac{d_2 + wl_2 p - \left(\alpha + b_1 \beta u\right) h(u)\frac{1}{z}}{b_2}\right)\right) p \\ \dot{z} = -b_2 z^2 \end{cases} \tag{4.49}$$

4.6   The dynamical system during the rationing of capital goods

When the profitability is high in both sectors, the demand of capital goods grows fast and may eventually exceed the productive capacity of the relative sector; this happens when the relative price p satisfies (4.20) and (4.21), but (4.22) does not hold.

4.6.1   Profit and investment in each sector

Thus we must compute the shares in total output of capital goods of both sectors, having in mind that the demand of the second sector is satisfied first. From the rationing condition and (3.29) and (4.43) we have

$$I_1 + I_2 = b_2 K_2. \tag{4.50}$$

The accumulated profits of the capital goods sector can be determined using the expression giving the accumulated profits in the second sector (see (3.23), (3.22), and (3.21))

$$\Pi_2^c = \left(1 - \frac{wl_2}{b_2}p\right) b_2 K_2 - (d_2 + \delta) K_2, \tag{4.51}$$

while (see (3.23)) gross investment I_2 carried out in the capital goods sector is given by

$$I_2 = \left(1 - \frac{wl_2}{b_2}p - \frac{d_2}{b_2}\right) b_2 K_2. \tag{4.52}$$

Comparing (4.52) and (4.50) we can determine also the gross investment I_1 in the consumption goods sector:

$$I_1 = (wl_2 p + d_2) K_2 \tag{4.53}$$

Now it is easy to find the evolutions of the fixed capital stocks K_1 and K_2 in both sectors; from (3.3) and (4.52) we get

$$\dot{K}_2 = (b_2 - wl_2 p - d_2 - \delta) K_2, \tag{4.54}$$

whereas from (4.53) and (3.3) again we get

$$\dot{K}_1 = -\delta K_1 + (wl_2 p + d_2) K_2. \tag{4.55}$$

Formulas (4.54) and (4.55) yield the evolution of the relative capitalization

$$\dot{z} = (b_2 - wl_2 p - d_2) z - (wl_2 p + d_2) z^2. \tag{4.56}$$

4.6.2   Evolution of the inventory level

The demand of consumption goods now is

$$D_1 = \frac{(wl_1up + d_1)\,K_1 + (wl_2p + d_2)\,K_2}{p}. \tag{4.57}$$

From the above equation (4.57), (4.55), and (4.24) we deduce the evolution equation for the inventory level

$$\dot{s} = \left(1 - \frac{wl_1}{b_1}\right)u + \delta s - \frac{d_1}{b_1 p} - \frac{wl_2p + d_2}{b_1 p}z\,(1 + b_1 ps). \tag{4.58}$$

The evolution equation for the relative price p can be deduced having in mind that

$$\frac{D_2 - Y_2}{Y_2} = \frac{(\alpha + b_1\beta u)\,h(u)K_1 - (wl_2p + d_2)\,K_2}{b_2 K_2} \tag{4.59}$$

4.6.3   The differential system

Finally we are in position to write the differential system of rationing for the four usual relative variables

$$\begin{cases} \dot{u} &=& F\,(u, s) \\ \dot{s} &=& \mathcal{G}^{\nabla}\,(u, s, p, z) \\ \dot{p} &=& \mathcal{H}^{\nabla}\,(u, p, z) \\ \dot{z} &=& \mathcal{K}^{\nabla}\,(u, s, p, z) \end{cases} \tag{4.60}$$

where:

$$\mathcal{G}^{\nabla}\,(u, s, p, z) = \left(1 - \frac{wl_1}{b_1}\right)u + \delta s - \tag{4.61}$$

$$\frac{d_1}{b_1 p} - \frac{wl_2 p + d_2}{b_1 p}z\,(1 + b_1 ps)$$

$$\mathcal{H}^{\nabla}\,(u, p, z) = \left[g_1\,(s) - g_2\left(\frac{(\alpha + b_1\beta u)\,h\,(u)}{b_2 z} - \right.\right. \tag{4.62}$$

$$\left.\left.\frac{wl_2 p + d_2}{b_2}\right)\right]p$$

$$\mathcal{K}^{\nabla}\,(u, s, p, z) = (b_2 - wl_2 p - d_2)\,z - (wl_2 p + d_2)\,z^2 \tag{4.63}$$

The differential system (4.60) describes the evolution of the system as long as the capital goods sector makes profits:

$$p \leq \frac{b_2 - d_2}{wl_2} \tag{4.64}$$

and the disequilibrium between demand and supply persists in the market for capital goods;

$$z \leq \frac{(\alpha + b_1\beta u)\,h\,(u)}{wl_2 + d_2} \tag{4.65}$$

Part II

Growth and Business Cycles

In this part we describe the evolution of the economy in absence of government interventions.

We first address the problem of the existence and stability of equilibrium points and describe the evolution of the system in an equilibrium point and in its vicinity (chapter 5). Then we pass to the analysis of the dynamics far from equilibrium and show that, when equilibrium is lost, a really complex dynamics emerges (chapter 6). Finally we present a discussion of how technical progress may perturb either equilibrium or disequilibrium dynamics (chapter 7).

5 Evolution of the Economy under Normal Conditions

In this chapter we describe the evolution of the economy when both sectors generate enough profit and the productivity capacity of the capital goods sector is sufficient to satisfy their demand.

5.1 Equilibrium points

Theorem 1 *The differential system (4.29) has an infinity of equilibrium points; all of them are of the form $(\bar{u}, \bar{s}, \bar{p}, \bar{z})$ where $\bar{u}$ and $\bar{s}$ are the normal values of the capacity utilization rate (3.15) and of the level of inventories (3.7) respectively and the equilibrium values for the relative price $\bar{p}$ and for the relative stock of fixed capital $\bar{z}$ satisfy (4.21), (4.22) and (4.23) and:*

$$\bar{z} = (b_2 - wl_2\bar{p}) \, \frac{\bar{\alpha} + b_1\bar{\beta}\bar{u}}{\left(\bar{\alpha} + b_1\bar{\beta}\bar{u}\right) wl_2\bar{p} + d_2b_2} \tag{5.1}$$

with $\bar{\alpha}$ and $\bar{\beta}$ evaluated at $\bar{p}$ and $\overline{k} = 1 + b_1\bar{s}\bar{p}$. All these equilibria are unstable[1].

We give a sketch of the proof in the mathematical appendix 19.3.

Remark 3 *Conditions (4.21), (4.22), and (4.23) may be given the form*

$$\bar{\alpha} + b_1\bar{\beta}\bar{u} > 0, \tag{5.2}$$

---

[1]It is clear that these equilibria are *ray equilibria*, i.e. equilibria in proportions, in the sense discussed by Boggio (1993)a.

$$b_2 - wl_2\bar{p} - d_2 \geqslant \bar{\alpha} + b_1\bar{\beta}\bar{u}, \tag{5.3}$$

$$\bar{p} \leqslant \frac{b_2 - d_2}{wl_2} \tag{5.4}$$

respectively.

Condition (5.2) is obviously satisfied if we make the quite natural hypothesis that the normal values $\bar{u}$ and $\bar{s}$ are chosen in such a way that the growth rate (4.9) of the consumption goods sector in the equilibrium point is non negative. If we put $\bar{p} = \bar{\alpha} + b_1\bar{\beta}\bar{u} - \delta$, the condition $\bar{p} \geqslant 0$ reads

$$\bar{u}\bar{p} > \frac{\delta + d_1}{b_1 - wl_1} \tag{5.5}$$

We observe that, when $b_2 - d_2 \geqslant wl_2\bar{p}$ and the condition (5.5) holds, in the equilibrium point we have

$$\frac{b_2 - d_2}{wl_2} > \frac{\delta + d_1}{b_1 - wl_1} \tag{5.6}$$

If this condition holds, then both (5.4) and (5.5) are satisfied and this means that a positive growth rate $\bar{p}$ of the consumption goods sector guarantees that the capital goods sector makes enough profit in order to pay the scheduled dividends (3.12), at least as long as the equilibrium value of the relative price p does not exceeds the upper bound (5.4).

Remark 4 *We complete this discussion writing condition (5.3) as an upper bound on the equilibrium value of the relative price $\bar{p}$; if we put*

$$\bar{\gamma} = b_2 - (\delta + d_1)\, b_1\bar{s} - wl_2 - (b_1 - wl_1)\,\bar{u}, \tag{5.7}$$

it is easy to prove that (5.3) is equivalent to the inequality

$$b_2 + \bar{\gamma}\bar{p} - wl_2 b_1\bar{s}\bar{p}^2 \geqslant 0 \tag{5.8}$$

Having in mind that the relative price $\bar{p}$ is obviously positive, condition (5.8) yields the upper bound

$$\bar{p} \leqslant \frac{\bar{\gamma} + \sqrt{\bar{\gamma}^2 + 4wl_2 b_1\bar{s}b_2}}{2wl_2 b_1\bar{s}} \tag{5.9}$$

5.2   Evolution of the system in a neighborhood of an equilibrium point

Since the matrix of the linearized system has a null eigenvalue, the linear approximation is unable to give information on the evolution of the system (4.29) near an equilibrium point (5.1); instead we use the adiabatic principle[2].

---

[2] We refer to Haken (1977), Haken (1983), and Zhang (1991).

5.2.1 Adiabatic approximation

In a neighborhood of an equilibrium point (5.1), the adiabatic approximation gives the following evolution

$$p = \frac{d_1}{\dfrac{\lambda_1 b_1}{\dfrac{\partial F(\bar{u}, \bar{s})}{\partial s}} \dfrac{F(u, s)}{1 - h(u)} + \delta b_1 s + (b_1 - w l_1)\, u} \tag{5.10}$$

Details of the proof of (5.10) may be found in the appendix 19.4.

Clearly equation (5.10) describes the evolution of the relative price p when the evolution of the capacity utilization rate u and the inventory level s are known, while equation (19.16) yields the evolution of the relative capitalization z.

Now it is worth noticing that, for any given initial condition for the relative price p, the projection on the (u, s) plane of the characteristic curves of the differential system (4.29) is qualitatively given by figure 5.1, independently of the initial condition for the relative capitalization z.

5.3   Expansion and depression

The preceding analysis suggests that the system may evolve according to two different regimes.

5.3.1 Expansion regime

The first one is characterized by a falling inventory level and an increasing capacity utilization rate; if the bounds (4.21), (4.22), and (4.23) did not hold, there would be a time $\tilde{t}$ such that

$$\begin{cases} \lim_{t \to \tilde{t}-} p(t) = +\infty \\ \lim_{t \to \tilde{t}-} s(t) = 0 \\ \lim_{t \to \tilde{t}-} u(t) = \tilde{u} \end{cases}, \tag{5.11}$$

where $\tilde{u}$ is the (unique) solution of the equation

$$(h(\tilde{u}) - 1)\, \tilde{u} = \frac{\lambda_1}{\left(1 - \dfrac{w l_1}{b_1}\right) \dfrac{\partial F(\bar{u}, \bar{s})}{\partial s}}\, F(\tilde{u}, 0). \tag{5.12}$$

Obviously $\bar{u} < \tilde{u} < 1$. Equation (5.12) can be easily obtained passing to the limit in (5.10). The hypothesis that $\lim_{s \to 0+} s g_1(s) = +\infty$ (see (3.8)),

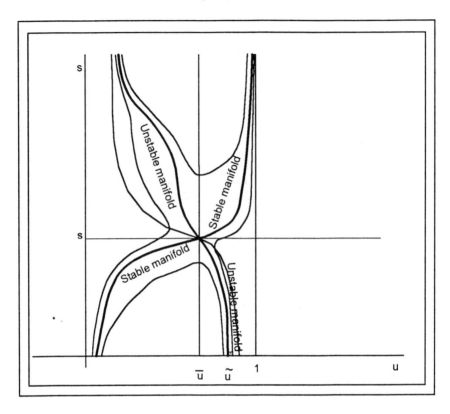

FIGURE 5.1. projection of the trajectories of the system in the u, s plane

together with $\lim\limits_{t \to \tilde{t}-} G\left(u(t), s(t), p(t)\right) = \left(1 - \frac{wl_1}{b_1}\right)\left(1 - h(\tilde{u})\right) \in R^+$, yields

$$\lim_{t \to \tilde{t}-} s(t)p(t) = +\infty. \tag{5.13}$$

We call this type of evolution expansion regime. The proofs of (5.11) and (5.13) are in the appendix 19.6.

5.3.2 Depression regime

The second type of asymptotic behavior of the solutions of the system (4.29) takes place when the inventory level rises while the capacity utilization rate falls; also in this case it is easy to prove that, if we again leave aside the bounds (4.21), (4.22), and (4.23), there exists a time $\widehat{t}$ such that

$$
\begin{cases}
\lim_{t \to \widehat{t}-} p(t) = 0 \\
\lim_{t \to \widehat{t}-} s(t) = +\infty \\
\lim_{t \to \widehat{t}-} u(t) = \widehat{u}
\end{cases}
, \tag{5.14}
$$

where $0 < \widehat{u} < \bar{u}$. Also in this case the condition $\lim_{s \to +\infty} g_1(s) = -\infty$ (see (3.8) again) yields

$$
\lim_{t \to \widehat{t}-} s(t)p(t) = 0. \tag{5.15}
$$

We call this alternative behavior depression regime. The following section is devoted to the analysis of this two alternative evolutions. The proofs of (5.14) and (5.15) are in appendix 19.5.

6 Depression and Expansion Regimes

We describe first the depression regime and pass then to treat the expansion one. We refer to figure 6.1 for a three dimension projection of the characteristic lines.

6.1 Evolution of the depression

6.1.1 The depression regime and the fall of profits

In this section we describe the evolution of the economy when a downturn begins.

We prove that the depression is bound to last and deepen more and more; it undermines the profitability of both sectors, but its effects are not uniform throughout sectors, since an unbalalce arises between the sectors and the profitability of the capital goods sector declines more rapidly.

The proof can be achieved showing that after some time the condition (4.21) no longer holds. This means that the contraction of the investment in the consumption goods sector causes an overcapitalization of the capital goods sector and its progressive loss of profitability.

Theorem 2 *If the initial conditions lead to a depression regime (5.14) (5.15), then there exists a time $\widehat{t_2}$ such that*

$$
\begin{array}{cc}
I_2(t) > 0 & \text{for} \quad t < \widehat{t_2} \\
& \text{and} \\
I_2(\widehat{t_2}) = 0 &
\end{array}
\tag{6.1}
$$

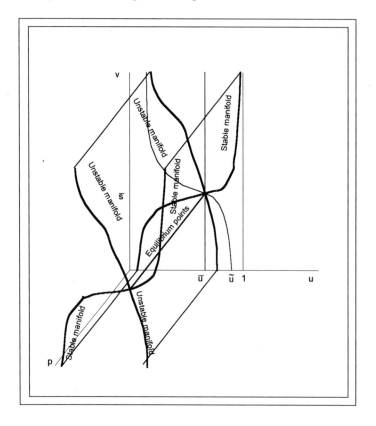

FIGURE 6.1. three dimensional projection of the stable and unstable manifolds of the system in the u, s, p space

The proof is postponed to the appendix 19.7.

Remark 5 *It is evident that instant $\hat{t}_2$ is the moment when investment in the capital goods sector ceases being profitable: the fall of the capacity utilization rate has caused a contraction of investment in the consumption goods sector resulting in an increasing excess of the productive capacity of the other sector, that eventually can not remunerate the fixed capital any longer.*

The decision to delay new investment in the consumption goods sector (i.e. the effect of the accelerator[1]) and the stop of investment in the capital goods sector may result in an accumulation of loanable funds in the further phase of the depression[2].

---

[1] See subsections 2.2.3, 3.2.3 and formulae (3.18), (3.19).

[2] See subsection 7.2.2 for a further and more comprehensive discussion on this point.

This fits perfectly a dynamics accounted for by the structural theories of the business cycle.. For instance Spiethoff (1925)[3] observes that "the accumulation of loanable funds proceeds in a continuous manner..., but the use of these funds in the form of productive investment is subject to fluctuations. ...During the depression, loanable funds find no outlet".

An empirical evidence for this had been provided by Tugan-Baranowskj[4]

Remark 6 *Since* $\lim_{t \to \hat{t}-} p(t) = 0$ *condition (4.23) surely holds during the depression, so rationing of the capital goods is excluded also in the time interval preceding instant* $\hat{t}_2$.

6.1.2   The system during the depression

After time $t = \hat{t}_2$ the evolution of the economy is no longer given by the differential system under normal conditions (4.29), but by the differential system of the falling profits (4.37).

The considerations which have led to (5.14), (5.15) and (19.24) hold also when the system is (4.37). The diminishing returns in the capital goods sector does not change the evolution of the depression: the fall of the relative price p and the increase of the inventory level s go on also after the instant $\hat{t}_2$ as long as the profitability of the consumption goods sector too peters out.

Theorem 3 *Under the assumptions of the preceding theorem, there exists a time* $\hat{t}_1 > \hat{t}_2$ *such that*

$$I_1^a(t) > 0 \quad for \quad t < \hat{t}_1$$
$$and$$
$$I_1^a(\hat{t}_1) = 0$$

(6.2)

The proof can be obtained as in the preceding case, having in mind (19.25) and (5.6).

After instant $\hat{t}_1$ both investment in the consumption and production in the capital goods sector come to an end together with the distribution of profits and the payment of wages in the second sector. On the contrary the production of consumption goods goes on since producing diminishes losses; dividends (3.12) are still distributed resorting to inventories.

---

[3] Cited after Hagemann and Landesmann (1998), p. 110.

[4] "In our study of individual recessions and crisis we have indicated the tremendous growth of the reserves of banks just after an economic crisis, when the economy is in recession. This indicates an accumulation of free capital which is not invested in industry." Tugan-Baranowskj (1894) cited after Hagemann and Landesmann (1998).

6.1.3   Existence of a turning point

After instant $\widehat{t}_1$ the evolution of the economy is described by the differential system of the slump (4.40)

From the third equation in (4.40) it is easy to see that the decline of the relative price continues also in a time interval following instant $\widehat{t}_1$, when the production of capital goods does not take place, since $s(t) > \overline{s}$ in a right neighborhood of that instant; however the second equation of (4.40), together with (5.15), proves that the inventory level increases up to an instant $\widehat{t}_0$ (with $\widehat{t}_0 > \widehat{t}_1$) , after which it begins to decline. The higher the level has gone up, the quicker its fall will be; it continues at least until eventually $s(t) = \overline{s}$; in this moment the fall of the relative price p stops and a new increase begins.

Also the capacity utilization rate stops falling a short time after instant $\widehat{t}_0$ and starts again increasing, while the inventory level declines. All these facts allow the system to approach one of the equilibrium points (5.1) again.

Remark 7 *We feel it is worth underlying that all these changes are completely endogenous to the system and we do not need to suppose either a change in agents' expectations or in their behavior in order that they take place.*

Remark 8 *In this point our model is definitely different from the theories which have inspired it.*

In Fanno (1931) either the beginning and the end of the depression are caused by sudden changes in agents' behavior, which the theory does not account for: the beginning is caused by an unexpected increase of the consumers' propensity to save, while the recovery starts 'When, for any reason, the ground is prepared for an upturn in the economy or an upturn is forecast, future profit rates will be forecast to rise and production increases are encouraged' (see sect.17). We find analogous considerations in Aftalion who states that the recovery starts when entrepreneurs begin somehow to expect future profits (see vol.. II page. 370 and following), whereas the evolution of expectations is outside the scope of theory.

In Tugan-Baranowski the economic crisis makes a readjustment of proportions by means of economic and social losses, providing the basis of the renewed expansion. In our model this amounts to assume that after the fall of profit in both sectors (say, for instance, after instant t_1, see theorem 3) a substantial sock of fixed capital is scraped in each sector and even a part of the inventories is lost, thus restoring better proportions and higher profitability. Of course this is a fully acceptable alternative assumption in the framework of our model and a different, but perfectly coherent endogenous mechanism generating the turning point. At the deepest point of the depression the demand may recover also because of an intervention of the government or an increase in foreign demand for exported commodities; we *shall address these exogenous causes of a recovery in part 3 and 4, respectively.*

Remark 9 *We note explicitly the second equation among (3.21) does not mean that inventories increase during the whole descending phase of the cycle; it means simply that, after a possible increase at the beginning of the downward phase, they decrease more slowly than productive capacity; since also the second equation of (3.18) must be interpreted in the same manner, it is evident that our model faithfully describes the evolution of inventories we find in Fanno's theory.*

Moreover it allows us to throw some light on the contrast between Fanno and Tugan-Baranowski (see Fanno (1931) sect. 16 and Footnote 25). It is clear that the important quantity for Tugan-Baranowski (1913) is not the absolute stock of inventories, but rather their relative level.

We conclude noticing that in our model a high inventory level allows the system to overcome the inferior turning point, but it is not the cause of the inversion of the cycle, as it is in Tugan-Baranowski; for a further discussion of this point we refer to the comments at the end of section 5.3.

6.2 Evolution of the expansion

6.2.1 Expansion and overheating

Now we move on to the analysis and the description of the expansion regime. When the relative price is boosted by a demand which exceeds supply of consumption goods and reduces inventories, the consumption goods sector increases its profits and its productive capacity as well, since expectations are in favor not only of a further increase of the demand, but even of a rate of growth exceeding the rate of growth of the capital goods sector. All this can be easily seen observing that formulas (5.13) and (5.11) yield

$$\begin{cases} \lim_{t \to \tilde{t}-} k(t) = +\infty \\ \lim_{t \to \tilde{t}-} \alpha(t) = \delta \\ \lim_{t \to \tilde{t}-} \beta(t) = +\infty \end{cases} ; \qquad (6.3)$$

thus the variation of the relative capitalization $\dot{z}$ soon becomes negative (we refer also to the last equation in system (4.29)).

In full analogy with the considerations which have led to the proof of the preceding theorem, we can show that condition (4.23) can not hold for every $t > 0$, when (6.3) holds. Hence there exists an instant $\tilde{t}_0$ such that either rationing of capital goods cannot be avoided, or the capital goods sector is no longer able to distribute the scheduled profits.

The first alternative occurs when the size of the consumption goods sector exceeds that of the capital goods sector so much that the latter has no longer enough production capacity in order to fully satisfy the demand for its products. In this case the capital goods sector turns out to be undercapitalized with respect to the other sector. In this case the expansion causes an overheating of the economy and significative price rises in both sectors.

The second alternative occurs when the price of the consumption goods reaches a so high level that the capital goods sector is no longer able to accumulate profits, moreover it is compelled to reduce the distributed part under the scheduled level. In this case the capital goods sector turns out to be overcapitalized with respect to the other sector. Thus a disequilibrium arises among profit rates of different sectors.

Remark 10 *We notice that both effects have been observed by theorists of the trade cycle since a long time as possible conclusions of the late phase of a recovery.*

In particular Bresciani-Turroni[5] contends Spiethoff's opinion that the fall of profits in the capital goods sector is the cause of the break down of the expansion phase. Here we show that both effects are possible and the occurrence of either the former or the latter depends on the relative sizes of the sectors at the beginning of the upturn.

This result, together with theorems 2 and 3, are in agreement with the empirically tested fact that the instrumental goods sector undergoes more severe oscillations during the business cycle than the consumption goods one[6]

6.2.2   The fall of profits in the capital goods sector

We begin examining the second alternative among those described above. The dynamical system is again given by (4.37); therefore the capacity utilization rate u, the inventory level s and the relative price p do not vary their evolutions after the instant $\tilde{t}_0$, while the relative capitalization further decreases. So there exists an instant $\tilde{t}_1 > \tilde{t}_0$ such that (4.22) does not hold for $t > \tilde{t}_1$ and rationing of capital goods begins. After instant $\tilde{t}_1$ ex post investment I_1 in the consumption goods sector equals the maximum productive capacity of the capital goods sector precisely, since in this sector no investment is taking place since instant $\tilde{t}_0$.

After instant $\tilde{t}_1$ the differential system (4.37) is replaced by the dynamical system of the disequilibrium in profit rates (4.49)

---

[5] See Bresciani-Turroni (1936) p. 163.

[6] The total volume of national production fluctuates only little from year to year...but even these small fluctuations are sufficient to generate violent oscillations in those industries which produce means of production (see Tugan-Baranowski (1901) p. 238).

The relative capitalization z and the inventory level s are on the decline, at least for a while, also after instant $\tilde{t}_1$, whereas the relative price p and the capacity utilization rate u go on increasing; however, within a certain time, either the right hand side of the second equation of (4.49) changes its sign, or the right hand side of the third equation of (4.49) changes its sign before that of the second one. In the first case the inventory level s enters a growth phase (while the capacity utilization rate u declines) up to a moment in which also the relative price p begins falling, since the term $g_1(s)$ is decreasing whereas the term $g_2\left(\frac{\bar{\alpha}+b_1\bar{\beta}\bar{u}}{b_2}h(u)\frac{1}{z} - 1\right)$ is still increasing. In the second case the relative price p begins falling. In any case we denote by $\tilde{t}_2$ the instant when either alternative occurs.

The first alternative occurs when the reaction (3.30) of the unitary price of the capital goods to the disequilibrium between supply and demand is not too strong: in this case, after instant $\tilde{t}_2$ the system is driven towards one of the equilibrium points (5.1). As in the case of depression, the regime described by system (4.49) has two different possible ends. Either the activity level of the consumption goods sector diminishes until the investment I_1^a planned by firms falls under the maximum productive capacity of the second sector again, so that we come back to the differential system (4.37); or the relative price of the consumption goods p falls so quickly that the capital goods sector recovers its profitability and can start investment again. The evolution of the system in the last case is described by the dynamical system of rationing (4.60). We are going to discuss it in the following subsection.

The profitability recover and the beginning of a new phase of investment in the capital goods sector after instant $\tilde{t}_2$ is the most probable outcome also when the second alternative prevails and thus we are led to the dynamical system (4.60) also in this case. The less probable outcome is that the evolution of the inventory level undergoes a change in direction so that the system is brought back to the situation described by (4.37).

6.2.3 Rationing

A first observation is in order: the evolution described by the dynamical system of rationing (4.60) is more complex than that we have analyzed in the cases of the former systems (4.37) and (4.49). Our first result is about the existence of a turning point in the rising trend of the relative price p.

Theorem 4 *There exists an instant $\tilde{t}_3 > \tilde{t}_0$ such that*
$\dot{p}(t) > 0$ *for* $\tilde{t}_3 < t$
and
$\dot{p}(t) < 0$ *for* $t > \tilde{t}_3$.

The proof is in the appendix 19.7.

Remark 11 *The length of the time interval $\left[\tilde{t}_0, \tilde{t}_3\right]$ obviously depends on the reaction function (3.30). If the reaction is sufficiently slow the relative price p will still rise for a long time after instant $\tilde{t}_0$ and will possibly reach the threshold (4.64) above which the capital goods sector is no longer profitable: in this case we shift to the differential system (4.49). However the most plausible assumption is that the reaction is fast enough to avoid the occurrence described above; if this is the case the relative price p will soon begin falling. An argument quite similar to that we used in the proof of the preceding theorem proves that, as the price decreases, function $\mathcal{H}^\nabla$ tends to become positive, thus improving the proportion between the stocks of capital in both sectors and allowing the ratio z to overcome the threshold (4.65); in this case the equilibrium on the capital goods market is restored.*

We observe also that, as the price p is large and the inventory level s is small, function $\mathcal{G}^\nabla (u, s, p, z) > 0$, thus after instant $\tilde{t}$ also the inventory level s tends to increase again, whereas the capacity utilization rate u begins to decrease. In this way the system is again driven toward one of the equilibrium points (5.1).

The further evolution may be two fold: if the inventory level is still below its target value, the economy approaches the equilibrium and then a new upswing begins. On the contrary, if the inventory level has grown during the rationing phase and soon after, a downturn begins and the eventual outcome of rationing is an overproduction crisis due to overcapitalization (see subsections 6.1.2 and 6.1.3).

6.2.4 Stationary disequilibrium

The evolution given by (4.60) has not only the outcome described above (i.e. the return toward the equilibria (5.1)). In fact we are going to prove that this differential system may have an equilibrium point.

Theorem 5 *If the constant $\tilde{u}$ that appears in (5.11) satisfies the condition*

$$\tilde{u} > \frac{(d_1 + \delta)\, wl_2}{(b_1 - wl_1)\,(b_2 - d_2 - \delta)} \tag{6.4}$$

the dynamical system of rationing has at least an equilibrium point

$$\left(\overline{u^\nabla}, \overline{s^\nabla}, \overline{p^\nabla}, \overline{z^\nabla}\right)$$

The proof is postponed to the appendix 19.8.

Remark 12 *Condition (6.4) is easily satisfied if the constant $\tilde{u}$, that appears in (5.11) is sufficiently close to 1; we anyway assume that this is the case. This solution is also unique if the equilibrium relative price in equilibrium p^∇ is not too large; precisely*

$$\overline{p^\nabla} < \frac{b_2 - (d_2 + \delta)}{wl_2} \tag{6.5}$$

In any case we denote with $(u(\overline{p^\nabla}), s(\overline{p^\nabla}))$ either the unique solution of the system (19.31) (19.32) or the solution such that the capacity utilization rate $\overline{u^\nabla}$ is larger and the inventory level $\overline{s^\nabla}$ is smaller; it is clear that solutions with $\overline{u^\nabla}$ small and $\overline{s^\nabla}$ large are not interesting for the overheating regime. Finally we substitute $(u(\overline{p^\nabla}), s(\overline{p^\nabla}))$ into equation (19.30) and determine the equilibrium relative price .

Remark 13 *The existence of at least a solution $\overline{p^\nabla}$ satisfying (4.64) and (6.5) and such that the corresponding equilibrium point $\left(\overline{u^\nabla}, \overline{s^\nabla}, \overline{p^\nabla}, \overline{z^\nabla}\right)$ satisfies (4.65) obviously depends on the particular form of the two functions g_1 and g_2 . We think that there is no point in specifying these conditions, as they have no significant economic interpretation. Instead we prefer to analyze the stability of this point, in the case it exists.*

We prove in the appendix 19.9 that, under suitable conditions, the equilibrium is locally attractive.

In this case the system may remain in an overheating regime and both prices p_1 e p_2 rise with the same rate of growth, while the capacity utilization rate remains over the desired target and the inventory level remains below its normal level. Last but not least the disequilibrium in the capital goods market never peters out. We call this situation overheating stationary disequilibrium.

7 Technical Progress and Economic Fluctuations

"After the Second World War...the careful emphasis of the earlier models on the interaction between industrial structural change and macroeconomic fluctuations and the rich discussion on the role...of expectation formation and shifts in the income distribution over different phases of the business cycle was lost"[1].

In this chapter we show how these interactions can be caught by the model developed so far: we deal with the evolution of the economy after an innovation of the production process is introduced in one of the two sectors.

We study possible increases in the profit rates and growth rate, shifts of the normal equilibrium points, of the thresholds that cause transitions from the dynamics under normal conditions to either that of the falling profits or to that of rationing the possible role of different expectations.

7.1   Different cases of technical progress

Since we are assuming perfect information, all entrepreneurs innovate at the same time; thus the introduction of the innovation displays its effects on all production processes existing at time, say $t = 0$, in the involved sector. This means that we are tackling with a more efficient organization

---

[1] See Hagemann and Landesmann (1998) p. 123.

of existing productive processes. Analytically this results in the shift of some parameters of the system.

We do not treat the introduction of a new production process requiring new type capital goods: in this case we ought to describe how the old type capital stock is substituted by the new type one and the effects of the innovation would involve only the latter.

7.1.1 Innovation and equilibria

We generally perform our analysis under the assumption that the innovation under discussion does not cause changes in the normal values for both the production capacity utilization rate and the inventory level.

Optimistic and pessimistic expectations

This assumption is adequate for increases of the productivity of labor, but is not to be taken for granted when an increase of the productivity of capital occurs. In this case it means that firms in the consumption goods sector are wanting to increase the inventories after they have achieved the increase in the productive capacity; this is certainly the case if an upturn is expected as a result of the

exploitation of the new opportunities (optimistic expectations).

However a different scenario is conceivable as well: if expectations are in some sense static (or pessimistic), since the inventories have been considered adequate up to time $t = 0$, they are considered adequate also afterwards, despite their level, measured in terms of the productive capacity, has shifted downwards.

Since in this case expectations are largely unpredictable, we assume that the occurrence of optimistic and pessimistic expectations is a random variable[2] and we are going to discuss both cases.

Employment

As far as production decisions are concerned, we assume that at time $t = 0$ no sudden fall occurs in the employment level in either sector. Any adjustment, whenever necessary, is gradually assured by the same mechanism of production, price, and investment decisions at work also when no innovation occurs (see subsections 3.2.3, 3.2.2, 3.3.2, and 3.3.3).

This assumption fits a usual situation: the innovation is introduced under the strong confidence that it is profitable, but it is often very difficult

---

[2]Random shifts from optimistic to pessimistic expectations and conversely are a commonplace in expectation driven business cycle theory. The uncertainty introduced by the innovation is largely sufficient to account for randomness in expectation formation.

For an up to date model, a discussion of this problem, and a list of refeences we refer to Evans Honkapoja and Romer (1998).

to decide a priori the best way of running the new type process. In the period following this introduction the profitability is assessed and possible adjustment are progressively performed.

Whether this assumption is acceptable depends on the institutional set-up of the labor market; obviously the alternative assumption of perfect downward elasticity of the labor market may be more adequate in some situations. We shall give some hints in this direction in the following sections.

As usual in such a context we use starred symbols to denote coefficients relative to the old type production technique, while we use symbols without the star when they denote coefficients of the new type production process.

7.2 An increase of labor productivity in the consumption goods sector

Coherently with the above convention, an increase in the labor productivity in the consumption goods sector means that, instead of (3.1), for $i = 1$ we have

$$
Y_1 = \begin{cases} \min \left\{ b_1 K_1, \dfrac{b_1}{l_1^*} L_1 \right\} & \text{for} \quad t < 0 \\[2ex] \min \left\{ b_1 K_1, \dfrac{b_1}{l_1} L_1 \right\} & \text{for} \quad t \geqslant 0 \end{cases}, \tag{7.1}
$$

where $l_1^* > l_1$. Hence at time $t = 0$ the (mean and marginal) productivity of labor in the consumption goods sector jumps from $\frac{b_1}{l_1^*}$ to $\frac{b_1}{l_1}$, while the mean and marginal productivity of capital remains unchanged at $b_1 = b_1^*$.

7.2.1 Normal equilibria

Since we are assuming that the normal values $\overline{u}$ and $\overline{s}$ are not perturbed by the change, the new equilibrium points have the same first two coordinates as the old ones

$$
\begin{aligned} \overline{u} &= \overline{u}^* \\ \overline{s} &= \overline{s}^*, \end{aligned} \tag{7.2}
$$

while the last two are generally different. Equation (5.1) may be put in the form

$$
\overline{z} = \frac{1 - w \dfrac{l_2}{b_2} \overline{p}}{w \dfrac{l_2}{b_2} \overline{p} + \dfrac{d_2}{\overline{\alpha} + b_1 \overline{\beta u}}}. \tag{7.3}
$$

From (4.5), (4.6), and (4.7) it is clear that α does not vary as l_1 varies, while β is a decreasing function of l_1; thus (7.3) shows that

$$\overline{p} = \overline{p}^* \implies \overline{z} > \overline{z}^* \tag{7.4}$$

Hence, if prices are to be held fixed, the equilibrium is preserved increasing the stock of fixed capital in the capital goods sector.

We remark explicitly that, if the system was in an equilibrium point (5.1) for $t < 0$, then

$$u(0) = \lim_{t \to 0-} \frac{L_1(t)}{l_1 K_1(t)} > \lim_{t \to 0-} \frac{L_1(t)}{l_1^* K_1(t)} = \overline{u}, \tag{7.5}$$

$$\overline{s}(0) = \overline{s}^*. \tag{7.6}$$

Hence the introduction of the innovation leads entrepreneurs in the capital goods sector to increase investment in order to adequate the capital stock to the new requirements; this fuels the demand of capital goods and primes an upturn. Now it is clear also the meaning of (7.4): the capital stock in the second sector has to be increased in order to cope with the upper jump of the demand.

7.2.2 Expansion and depression

If the system was already experiencing an upswing before the introduction of the innovation at time $t = 0$, this accelerate the process.

Analytically $\lim_{t \to 0-} \alpha(t) = \alpha(0)$, while $\lim_{t \to 0-} \beta(t) < \beta(0)$; hence the right hand side of (4.25) has an downward jump at time $t = 0$, due to the upward jump of the second factor and the downward jump of the third factor.

Thus after $t = 0$ the inventory level shrinks more quickly. This in turn causes a quicker rise of the price p_1 of consumption goods; moreover, the threshold under which rationing of capital goods occurs shifts upwards. In fact now the capital goods sector is undercapitalized and hence rationing is more probable (see again (7.4)), as well as the eventual overheating.

We pass now to the analysis of the impact of the innovation on a system experiencing a fall in economic activity before time $t = 0$.

This is of a peculiar interest because the depression itself may be one of the determinants of the introduction of a technical innovation. Actually, as long as the depression deepens more and more entrepreneurs decide to delay new investment[3]; thus more and more loanable funds accumulate and the rate of interest declines. This is in general a vicious circle since the less investment is realized, the lower is the activity level of the system, the lower the profitability of firms in both sectors.

---

[3]This is the accelerator hypothesis discussed in subsection 2.2.3.

We have already discussed the problem of accumulation of loanable funds during the depression in subsection 6.1.1.

If a technical progress gives the opportunity of rising the profit rate, the vicious circle can be broken, precisely thanks to the low interest rate that makes "the exercise of the option to invest"[4] especially attractive. This is precisely the scenario offered by our model, soon after the innovation.

The upward jump of the productive capacity utilization rate (7.5) pushes the economy towards a normal equilibrium and may even drive it to an upturn, provided the upward jump is sufficiently wide.

Even if this is not the case, the further evolution of the depression phase is now much slower. Moreover the threshold, over which the capital goods sector is no longer profitable (see (4.21)), undergoes an upward shift, while the threshold, under which also profits of the consumption goods sector is undermined (see (4.20)), jumps downwards; thus the critical phase of the slump is delayed more and more.

We remark explicitly that at time $t = 0$ the employment in the capital goods sector increases, since $\lim_{t \to 0-} L_2(t) < L_2(0)$; this is due to the increase of investment in both sectors and means that the technological unemployment can be avoided in the present case thanks to the rise of the profitability of both sectors, which allows an increase of investment and thus results in an increase of the demand for labor.

We conclude this subsection stressing that the profit rate rises in both sectors because of the innovation. From formulas (19.4) and (19.7) it is easy to obtain the increase in a normal equilibrium point (5.1)

$$\overline{r}_1 - \overline{r}_1^* = \overline{r}_2 - \overline{r}_2^* = \frac{w\left(l_1^* - l_1\right)\overline{up}}{b_1\,\overline{sp} + 1}. \tag{7.7}$$

It is clear that in equilibrium the increase does not depend on the sector and is larger the larger is the productivity gain.

Outside normal equilibria the two rates generally have different increases: they depend on the different impact of the innovation on different sectors: if $\lim_{t \to 0-} u(t) = u^*$, at time $t = 0$ from formulas (19.3) and (19.7) we obtain

$$r_1 - r_1^* = \frac{(b_1 - wl_1)\,p\,(u - u^*) + w\left(l_1^* - l_1\right)up}{k_1} \tag{7.8}$$

$$r_2 - r_2^* = \frac{b_2 - wl_2p}{wl_2p} \tag{7.9}$$

$$\left(\frac{\alpha + b_1\beta u}{z}\left(h(u) - h(u^*)\right) + \frac{(b_1 - wl_1)\,p\,(u - u^*)}{z} + \right.$$

$$\left. \frac{w\left(l_1 - l_1^*\right)u^*p}{z} \right)$$

This result is not surprising because the profitability of the capital goods sector is obviously higher, the higher is the demand of capital goods gen-

---

[4] See subsection 2.2.3 again and the citations from Dixit and Pindyck (1994) there.

erated by the consumption goods sector and hence the higher is its profitability.

Also the growth rate of the economy in a normal equilibrium rises after the introduction of the innovation (see 4.10).

7.3   An increase of capital productivity in the consumption goods sector

Here we assume that the innovation, introduced at time $t = 0$, rises the productivity of capital in the consumption goods sector, while the labor productivity remains unchanged. Formally this means

$$
Y_1 = \begin{cases} \min\left\{b_1^* K_1, \dfrac{b_1^*}{l_1^*} L_1\right\} & \text{for} \quad t < 0 \\[3mm] \min\left\{b_1 K_1, \dfrac{b_1}{l_1} L_1\right\} & \text{for} \quad t \geqslant 0 \end{cases} , \tag{7.10}
$$

where $b_1^* < b_1$ and $\frac{b_1^*}{l_1^*} = \frac{b_1}{l_1}$. In this case it is easy to see that, at time $t = 0$, β decreases while α increases (see again (4.5), (4.6), and (4.7)).

The effect of this change on the normal equilibria (5.1) is opposite to that produced by the increase of the labor productivity discussed before; in fact

$$
\bar{p} = \bar{p}^* \Longrightarrow \bar{z} < \bar{z}^* \tag{7.11}
$$

7.3.1   Normal equilibria

Optimistic expectations

We start our analysis assuming that the economy was in a normal equilibrium before $t = 0$, maintaining the hypothesis that the innovation does not modify the normal values (7.2) and that the employment does not shrinks suddenly. In these assumptions it is easy to see that the capacity utilization rate u jumps downward at time $t = 0$

$$
u(0) = \lim_{t \to 0-} \frac{L_1(t)}{l_1 K_1(t)} < \lim_{t \to 0-} \frac{L_1(t)}{l_1^* K_1(t)} = \lim_{t \to 0-} u(t) = \bar{u}^*, \tag{7.12}
$$

(see (3.13)).

An analogous downward jump characterizes the evolution of the inventory level at the same time

$$
s(0) = \lim_{t \to 0-} \frac{S_1(t)}{b_1 K_1(t)} < \lim_{t \to 0-} \frac{S_1(t)}{b_1^* K_1(t)} = \lim_{t \to 0-} s(t) = \bar{s}^*. \tag{7.13}
$$

It is apparent that suitable production decisions (in the sense of subsection 2.2.2) allows to drive the economy towards a normal equilibrium, moving it along the stable manifold. An obvious strategy to pursue this aim is to increase the production capacity utilization rate and the price of consumption goods in order to set up inventories again.

It is not to be given for granted that these stabilizing choices are compatible with the decision criteria followed before the innovation: some adjustment may be necessary and in this sense we have possibly to allow an exception to our assumption that normal values and decision rules are not modified by the innovation.

On the other hand it is by no means obvious that entrepreneurs are able to implement exactly the strategy allowing the system to converge along the stable manifold, even if they are pursuing convergence. If this is not the case the economy may either accelerate too much and fall into an overheating phase, or begin to accumulate involuntary stocks with falling prices and declining output. The first case occurs when the increase of the production capacity utilization rate is insufficient to restore stocks, while the second one occurs if the additional productive capacity of the consumption goods sector is exploited too quickly, eventually causing an overproduction crisis.

Pessimistic expectations

Now we briefly discuss the alternative assumption to (7.2). Since the inventories $S(t)$ have been considered at their normal value for every $t < 0$, also $S(0)$ are considered at their normal value at $t = 0$. Formally this means

$$
\begin{aligned}
\bar{u} &= \bar{u}^* \\
\bar{s} &= \frac{b_1^*}{b_1}\bar{s}^*.
\end{aligned}
\tag{7.14}
$$

In this case the increase of the productive capacity in the first sector results in an initial increase of the output of consumption goods. However the demand does not increase proportionally because of a moderate propensity to invest; thus involuntary stockpiling begins, again priming an overproduction crisis.

The above discussion takes to the fore the problem of stock equilibrium during the traverse following a technical change. The chance of exploiting the increase of productive capacity without causing an overproduction crisis depends crucially on the impact of the innovation on the decision criteria and parameters that determine production, price, and investment decisions of firms.

If these are suitable a new equilibrium can be reached with higher profit and growth rates. However a probable outcome of the innovation process is the perturbation of the equilibrium and the begin of an instability phase with an eventual overproduction crisis.

It is to be noted that the pessimistic expectations are a typical example of self-fulfilling prophecy, while this is not necessarily always true for the optimistic ones.

7.3.2 Expansion and depression

To avoid a too long enumeration of cases, we restrict our description of the dynamic outside the equilibrium to the case when hypothesis (7.14) holds.

If the economy was experiencing a downswing before time $t = 0$, this remains true also after the innovation occurs. Writing (4.25) in the present case we obtain

$$
\dot{s} = \begin{cases} \left(s\delta + \left(1 - \dfrac{wl_1^*}{b_1^*}\right) u - \dfrac{d_1}{pb_1^*} \right)(1 - h(u)) & \text{for } t < 0 \\[3mm] \left(s\delta + \left(1 - \dfrac{wl_1}{b_1}\right) u - \dfrac{d_1}{pb_1} \right)(1 - h(u)) & \text{for } t \geqslant 0 \end{cases} . \tag{7.15}
$$

It is easy to see from (7.15) that the growth of the level of inventories slows down after $t = 0$. On the other hand the threshold determining the fall of profitability of the capital goods sector is now higher than before, whereas the threshold is lower, under which the price p is insufficient to allow the consumption goods sector to generate profits.

Hence the evolution of the economy toward the crisis is slower than before, both because of the slower involuntary stockpiling and because of the higher profitability of existing production processes that allows both sectors to generate higher profits.

On the contrary, if the economy was in an expansion phase before time $t = 0$, the innovation causes a slower depletion of inventories of consumption goods, but a faster rise of their price p_1 together with an increase of the threshold under which rationing begins. It is far from obvious ascertain which of these contrasting effects prevails: it depends on the initial conditions and parameters of the system whether the upper turning point is reached before or after the instant it would have reached it if the innovation had not occurred.

We conclude this subsection observing that also in this case both sectors benefit by an increase of the respective profit rates; from (19.3) and (19.7) we obtain

$$
r_1 - r_1^* = \frac{b_1 - b_1^*}{k_1} \left(1 - w\frac{l_1^*}{b_1^*}\right) pu \tag{7.16}
$$

$$
r_2 - r_2^* = \left(\frac{b_2}{wl_2 p} - 1\right) h(u)\,(b_1 - b_1^*)\left(1 - w\frac{l_1^*}{b_1^*}\right) pu \tag{7.17}
$$

From (7.16) and (7.17) it is plain that both sectors have the same increase when the economy is in a normal equilibrium point (5.1)

$$
\bar{r}_1 - \bar{r}_1^* = \bar{r}_2 - \bar{r}_2^* = \frac{b_1 - b_1^*}{\bar{k}_1} \left(1 - w\frac{l_1^*}{b_1^*}\right) \overline{pu} \tag{7.18}
$$

Formula (7.18) is analogous to (7.7).

Also the equilibrium growth rate of the economy rises after the introduction of the innovation.

7.4 An increase of labor productivity in the capital goods sector

Maintaining the notation introduced above, we assume that

$$
Y_2 = \begin{cases} \min\left\{ b_2 K_2, \dfrac{b_2}{l_2^*} L_2 \right\} & \text{for} \quad t < 0 \\[2mm] \min\left\{ b_2 K_2, \dfrac{b_2}{l_2} L_2 \right\} & \text{for} \quad t \geqslant 0 \end{cases}, \tag{7.19}
$$

where $l_2 < l_2^*$. In analogy with the case examined in section 7.2, at time $t = 0$ the (mean and marginal) productivity of labor in the capital goods sector jumps from $\frac{b_2}{l_2^*}$ to $\frac{b_2}{l_2}$, while the (mean and marginal) productivity of capital in the capital goods sector $b_2 = b_2^*$ remains unchanged.

7.4.1 Normal equilibria

Also in this case we are assuming that the normal values do not change because of the innovation. Thus the new equilibrium point has the same first two coordinates as before, while the third and forth ones are in general different. Equation (7.3) shows that

$$
\frac{\partial \bar{z}}{\partial l_2} = \frac{-w\bar{p}}{wl_2\bar{p} + \dfrac{d_2 b_2}{\bar{\alpha} + b_1 \overline{\beta u}}} - \frac{b_2 - wl_2\bar{p}}{\left(wl_2\bar{p} + \dfrac{d_2 b_2}{\bar{\alpha} + b_1 \overline{\beta u}} \right)^2} w\bar{p} < 0 \tag{7.20}
$$

Hence also in this case we have

$$
\bar{p} = \bar{p}^* \implies \bar{z} > \bar{z}^*. \tag{7.21}
$$

This again means that, with fixed prices, the equilibrium can be preserved increasing the relative size of the capital goods sector.

On the other hand the innovation itself fosters such a process; in fact at time $t = 0$ it becomes possible to satisfy the demand of capital goods coming from the consumption goods sector as before and to increase the amount of capital goods supplied to the capital goods sector, without increasing the labor employed in the sector itself. Formally we observe that $\lim_{t \to 0-} L_2(t) = L_2(0)$ while $\lim_{t \to 0-} Y_2(t) < Y_2(0)$.

Therefore, if the system was in a normal equilibrium (5.1) before time $t = 0$, then $u(t)$, $s(t)$, $p(t)$ remain constant also for $t > 0$, whereas $z(t) \to \bar{z}$ thanks to (4.27); in this case the new equilibrium is reached asymptotically.

7.4.2 Expansion and depression

Now we pass to the discussion of the effects of the innovation when at time $t = 0$ the economy was not in equilibrium.

Assuming again that the normal values do not vary (7.2), if the system was directed towards a depression for $t < 0$, this remains true also for $t \geqslant 0$; also the evolution of the inventory level is not immediately affected by the change because the right hand side of (4.25) is continuous at $t = 0$, as well as the right hand side of (5.1). However, after time $t = 0$, the threshold, under which the relative price p is too low and do not allow firms in the consumption goods sector to generate profit, increases, just as in the preceding case. Otherwise at time $t = 0$ there is no change in the threshold over which the capital goods sector does not produce profit; hence the first phase of the depression has the same evolution as before, but successively the turning point is reached sooner than if the innovation had not taken place.

There is no change at time $t = 0$ in the decline of the inventory level s and in the increase of the price of consumption goods p_1 also when the economy was experiencing an expansionary cycle before the innovation. However a rise occurs in the threshold over which the output of capital goods is insufficient to cope wit the demand and rationing begins; thus the innovation makes the expansion longer and the peak higher that before.

We conclude noticing that the innovation does not affects the rates of profit in equilibrium in either sector

$$\bar{r}_1 = \bar{r}_1^* \qquad (7.22)$$
$$\bar{r}_2 = \bar{r}_2^*$$

Whereas outside the equilibrium the rate of profit of the first sector does not vary, but that of the second sector jumps upwards

$$\begin{cases} r_1(0) = \lim_{t \to 0} r_1(t) \\ r_2(0) > \lim_{t \to 0-} r_2(t) \end{cases} , \qquad (7.23)$$

the height of the jump is given by

$$\frac{b_2}{wp} \left(\frac{1}{l_2} - \frac{1}{l_2^*} \right) \left(\frac{\alpha + b_1 \beta u}{z} h(u) - d_2 \right) \qquad (7.24)$$

Expression (7.24) is positive because of (4.18)

Also the growth rate of the economy in equilibrium does not vary after the innovation.

7.5 An increase of the capital productivity in the capital goods sector

Using once more the notation introduced above, the increase of the productivity of capital in the capital goods sector is formally expressed in the following form

$$
Y_2 = \begin{cases} \min\left\{ b_2^* K_2, \dfrac{b_2^*}{l_2^*} L_2 \right\} & \text{for} \quad t < 0 \\[3mm] \min\left\{ b_2 K_2, \dfrac{b_2}{l_2} L_2 \right\} & \text{for} \quad t \geqslant 0 \end{cases} , \qquad (7.25)
$$

where $b_2^* < b_2$, while $\frac{b_2^*}{l_2^*} = \frac{b_2}{l_2}$. As in the case discussed in subsection 7.3 (see (7.10)), the (mean and marginal) productivity of labor does not change in the capital goods sector, while the (mean and marginal) productivity of capital increases from b_2^* to b_2.

7.5.1 Normal equilibria

If we maintain the assumption (7.2) that no change occurs in the normal values, it is easy to realize that the normal equilibria (5.1) do not vary. Moreover the introduction of the innovation does not affect the dynamical system under normal conditions (4.29) and therefore no change occurs in the evolution of the system near normal equilibrium points.

7.5.2 Expansion and depression

No shift occurs in the threshold (4.21) under which the capital goods sector looses its profitability; thus, if the system was directed toward a downturn before the innovation, its evolution does not chance afterwards. This is a quite natural result, since the unused productive capacity increases in the capital goods sector during the depression more and more and such increase can obviously not revert the trend.

A more interesting situation arises when the system was in an expansion phase before the innovation. It is easy to see that in this case rationing of capital goods become less probable after time $t = 0$, because of the downward shift of the threshold (4.22) under which firms in the capital goods sector are unable to satisfy the demand

$$
\frac{\alpha + b_1 \beta u}{w l_2^* p + d_2} h\left(u\right) > \frac{\alpha + b_1 \beta u}{w l_2 p + d_2} h\left(u\right). \qquad (7.26)
$$

Hence the recovery is longer than before since the increase of the productive capacity in the capital goods sector prevents price rises in this sector, at least for a certain time after the innovation; the peak is higher and later.

Also the compatibility condition (4.23) on the nominal wage rate is less binding and the nominal wage may reach a higher level than before.

The rates of profit do not change in either sector.

Remark 14 *In this case and in the preceding one the increases of productivity in the capital goods sector do not generally affect the profit rates; this* *is perfectly natural if we take into account that the numeraire of our model is the physical unit of capital good, thanks to our choice of the normalization of prices.*

Because of this choice, when the productivity of capital increases the price of an efficiency unit of capital decreases. When the increase takes place in the consumption goods sector the profit rate of this sector rises and pulls up the profit rate in the other sector too; when the increase takes place in the capital goods sector the two effects compensate each other.

Obviously we could make different assumptions and choose the efficiency unit of capital as numeraire; in this case an increase of the capital productivity would cause a parallel rise of the price p_2 of the physical unit of capital. We do not dwell into this problem any longer as we do not think that the interest in this case is worth a necessarily complex discussion.

There is a second point to be stressed: after a productivity increase in the capital goods sector expansion phases are longer and peak higher than before. This means that, if the economy was in an expansionary phase before date $t = 0$, the average growth rate after $t = 0$ is higher than it would have been if the innovation had not been introduced.

Part III

Stabilization Policies

In this part we discuss the role of the government in our model. First we describe the problems we want to discuss and state the hypotheses under which we are going to treat them (chapter 8).

Second we provide an analytic framework (chapter 9) in which relevant policy issues are addressed; in particular we describe equilibrium positions when the government balances its budget (chapter 10).

Third we pass to the discussion of some anti-inflationary strategies (chapter 11) and conclude examining possible expansionary policies (chapter 12).

8 Unstable Growth Paths and Effectiveness of Fiscal Policies

8.1   Instability in multisector models

The problem of the instability of the steady state growth path and the emergence of either cyclical or complex oscillatory trajectories affects multisectorial growth models notwithstanding their possible completely different theoretical foundations.

After the pioneering attempts due to Kaldor[1], Hicks[2], and Goodwin[3], the first path-breaking result in this direction is Hahn's well known proof that the balanced growth path is a saddle point in the neo-classical multisectorial growth model[4]; beside it we remember only few results in this direction as Burmeister et al.[5], Burmeister[6], and Kuga[7]. After Goodwin's basic result[8] on the endogenously generated business cycle, many other interesting cases have come to the fore, among them we remember only those

---

[1] See Kaldor (1940); for further developments we refer also to Chang and Smith (1971) and Asada (1987).

[2] See Hicks (1950).

[3] See Goodwin (1951).

[4] See Hahn (1966).

[5] See Burmeister Caton Dobell and Ross (1973).

[6] See Burmeister (1980).

[7] See Kuga (1977).

[8] See Goodwin (1967).

due to Grandmont[9] and Woodford[10], obtained assuming perfect competition and perfect foresight, and those due to Benhbib and Nishimura[11] and to Nishimura and Yano[12], to which we refer also for a rich list of bibliographical references.

As far as the modern formulation of the classical competition process is concerned, Boggio[13] has proved the instability of the steady state growth path in the so called "pure cross-dual model"; in particular he has shown that proportions among sectors are stable whereas their dimensions are unstable. This result parallels in some sense the dual instability exhibited by the dynamic Leontief model: here stability of quantities implies instability of prices and conversely[14].

8.1.1   Does fiscal policy matter?

In this connection a crucial question is whether the government can and should take actions designed to influence key economic variables such as inflation and unemployment and, if this is the case, what kind of measures will achieve the desired results. For both a thorough discussion of the problem and for a review of the existing literature we refer to the classical paper by Blinder and Solow[15].

In this part we want to discuss the effectiveness of some stabilizing fiscal policies in the framework of the model presented in part I. Our focus is on global policies directed at influencing the overall level of government expenditures, the overall level of taxes, or the size of government budget deficit; so we disregard the problem of "fine tuning" the economic system.

8.2   The Role of the Government

Since the focus of this part is on the effectiveness of government spending and taxation to stabilize the economic system, we begin the description of the model fixing ideas on the main features of the alternative government actions we are going to assess in the following sections.

---

[9] See Grandmont (1985).

[10] See Woodford (1994).

[11] See Benhabib and Nishimura (1979).

[12] See Nishimura and Yano (1995)a, see also Nishimura and Yano (1995)b and Nishimura and Yano (1995)b.

[13] See Boggio (1993)a. In this respect we refer also to Boggio (1993)b and to Dumenil and Levy (1989).

[14] See again Jorgenson (1961), Burmeister and Dobell (1970), and Aoki (1977).

[15] See Blinder and Solow (1973).

8.2.1 Government spending

As far as government spending is concerned, we first assume that the government does not directly engage in productive activities since it is a widespread belief that public sector outlays on business fixed investment simply crowd out potential analogous private outlays, without altering the aggregate levels of output and employment; we refer to the recent paper of Aschauer[16] for further details.

Thus we shall consider two types of government spending: purchases of goods and services on the consumption goods market and direct transfers to households. As far as transfers are concerned, in what follows our interest focuses on unemployment benefits to be paid during slumps.

8.2.2 Profit tax and consumption tax

Our second key hypothesis is that deficit spending (or surplus) is allowed, provided it is temporary and possibly either followed or preceded by a surplus (deficit) phase. In equilibrium the government is assumed to balance its budget levying either consumption taxes or profit taxes or both of them (see chapter 10.1.3).

Unless otherwise stated we assume proportional taxes. Tax rates may be either fixed or variable and the government may decide to link their variations to those of some relevant economic variable such as the inflation rate.

We are going to discuss two different types of government intervention.

- The first one seeks to stimulate the economy when it enters a depression regime, to lower unemployment, and to increase real income; it may take different forms such as tax cuts or increased transfers (see chapter 12).

- The second one seeks to hold the economy back in a boom, to prevent overheating and lower the inflation rate. The intervention consists of increases of taxation: we are going to examine different alternatives of these increases (see chapter 11).

---

[16] See Aschauer (1988).

9 Further Equations

9.1 The government

This chapter is devoted to the introduction of suitable equations describing the assumptions on government actions examined in the preceding one (chapter 8).

9.1.1 Profit tax

Let us denote by T^p the revenue of the profit tax and by t^p the corresponding tax rate. We still denote by Π_i the before tax net profit generated by the i-th sector (3.10) (3.21), then the after tax profit is

$$\Pi_i^n = (1 - t^p)\,\Pi_i. \tag{9.1}$$

The after tax profit is then divided into two parts, one for consumption Π_i^c and the other for accumulation Π_i^a and hence (compare (9.2) with (3.12) and (3.23), having in mind (3.12) and (3.22))

$$\Pi_i^n = \Pi_i^c + \Pi_i^a. \tag{9.2}$$

Thus the revenue of the profit tax is

$$T^p = t^p\,(\Pi_1 + \Pi_2)\,. \tag{9.3}$$

9.1.2   *Government spending*

Coming now to government spending, it may be split into two components[1]: direct purchases P on the market of consumption goods and direct transfers B to households.

Since we are assuming that workers have no propensity for saving, it is natural to suppose that households spend the whole amount of direct transfers B on the consumption goods market.

9.1.3   *Consumption tax*

If we still denote by W_i the total wages of workers employed in the i-th sector, the revenue of the consumption tax is

$$T^c = t^c \left(W_1 + W_2 + \Pi_1^c + \Pi_2^c + B + P \right). \tag{9.4}$$

We remember that worker's propensity for saving is null.

Remark 15 *We may alternatively assume that government purchases on the consumption goods market are tax free; in this different assumption (9.4) must be replaced by*

$$T^c = t^c \left(W_1 + W_2 + \Pi_1^c + \Pi_2^c + B \right). \tag{9.5}$$

We shall briefly develope this case (see remarks 16 and 17).

9.2   The consumption goods sector

The intervention of the government does not directly affect the income of workers in the sector (3.4), the price decisions of firms (3.8), the conditions of profitability of the sector (3.6) (3.9), and the before tax profit (3.10), as well as the evolution of inventories (3.9), the decisions to produce (3.16) (3.28), and to invest (3.2) (3.19) (3.18).

Also in this case we express the dynamics of the economy in terms of the productive capacity utilization rate u (3.15), the inventory level s (3.7), the relative price p (3.30), and the relative capitalization z (4.1).

9.2.1   *The demand*

The demand for consumption goods, D_1, is the sum of workers' demand, capitalists' demand, government spending on consumer goods, and the de-

---

[1] We recall that we are assuming that the government does not engage directly in productive activities

mand generated by government transfers, minus the consumption tax

$$D_1 = \frac{\Pi_1^c + \Pi_2^c + W_1 + W_2 + P + B - T^c}{p_1}. \qquad (9.6)$$

9.2.2 Profits, investment, and growth

Concerning the profits allocated to consumption we still assume that this part is proportional to the value of the stock of productive capital of the sector; therefore:

$$\Pi_1^c = d_1 K_1 p_2, \qquad (9.7)$$

where $d_1 > 0$ is the dividend normally paid by firms in the consumption goods sector.

The accumulated profit in the first sector may be computed substituting (3.1), (3.4) into (3.10) and the result into (9.2)

$$\Pi_1^a = (1 - t^p) \Pi_1 - \Pi_1^c = \left[(1 - t^p) \left(\left(1 - \frac{wl_1}{b_1} \right) pb_1 u - \delta \right) \right] K_1 - d_1 K_1. \qquad (9.8)$$

Comparing equations (4.4) and (9.8) shows clearly how Π_1^a is affected by the introduction of the profit tax. We stress the point that the accumulated profit, Π_1^a (see also (9.2)), need not be positive.

If we set

$$\beta_{t^p} = \frac{1}{k} \left(1 - \frac{wl_1}{b_1} \right) p (1 - t^p) \qquad (9.9)$$

$$\alpha_{t^p} = \delta - \frac{d_1 + \delta (1 - t^p)}{k} \qquad (9.10)$$

and insert (9.8) into (3.18), we obtain the ex ante investment in the consumption goods sector in terms of the coefficients (9.9) and (9.10)

$$I_1^a = \max \left\{ (\alpha_{t^p} + b_1 \beta_{t^p} u) h (u) K_1, 0 \right\}. \qquad (9.11)$$

Finally, if we denote the growth rate of the fixed capital stock of the consumption goods sector by ρ_{t^p} then from (3.3) and (9.11) we can write

$$\dot{K}_1 = \rho_{t^p} K_1, \qquad (9.12)$$

with

$$\rho_{t^p} = (\alpha_{t^p} + b_1 \beta_{t^p} u) h (u) - \delta. \qquad (9.13)$$

Formulae (9.12) and (9.13) have to be compared with (4.9) and (4.10) respectively. In particular it is apparent that only the profit tax (9.3) affects the rate of growth ρ_{t^p} of the consumption goods sector; since in normal conditions $\left(1 - \frac{wl_1}{b_1} \right) p > \delta$ the overall effect of the profit tax is to depress the growth rate.

9.3 The capital goods sector

At the formal level, the effects of government intervention on the capital goods sector are similar to those on the consumption goods sector under many respects.

Also in this case there are no direct changes in the income of workers in the sector (3.20), the price decisions of firms (3.30), the conditions of profitability of the sector (3.25) (3.26), and the before tax profit (3.21), the decisions to produce (3.24) and to invest (3.32). In this case also the demand for capital goods (3.27) is not directly affected by government spending, since we are assuming that the government does not make direct purchases of productive plants.

We still assume that firms in this sector pay a fixed dividend d_2 for the capital invested there, at least as long as their profits are sufficient; hence the consumed part of profit is again given by

$$\Pi_2^c = \min \{d_2 K_2 p_2, Y_2 p_2 - W_2\}. \tag{9.14}$$

9.3.1 Profits, investment, output, and total wages

As far as the capital goods sector is concerned, if dividends can be regularly distributed (3.31), the accumulated profit of the second sector can be obtained following the lines which led to (9.8) for the first sector

$$\Pi_2^a = (1 - t^p) \left(1 - \frac{wl_2}{b_2}p\right) Y_2 - (d_2 + \delta (1 - t^p)) K_2. \tag{9.15}$$

Substituting (9.15) into (3.32) we can determine the gross investment in the capital goods sector

$$I_2 = \max \left\{(1 - t^p) \left(1 - \frac{wl_2}{b_2}p\right) Y_2 - (d_2 - \delta t^p) K_2, 0\right\}. \tag{9.16}$$

On the other hand, from the condition of non-negativity of output, $Y_2 \geq 0$, from (3.27) (3.28) (3.29) of section 3.3.2 and (9.16) we can write Y_2 in terms of the investment I_1 in the first sector and the capital stock K_2 in the second one

$$Y_2 = \max \left\{\frac{1}{1 - \left(1 - \frac{wl_2}{b_2}p\right)(1 - t^p)} (I_1 - (d_2 - \delta t^p) K_2), 0\right\}. \tag{9.17}$$

Assuming that the productive capacity of the capital goods sector is sufficient (see condition 9.21 below) to avoid rationing (i.e. $I_1 = I_1^a$), we can determine the output of capital goods simply introducing (9.11) into (9.17) and obtaining

$$Y_2 = \frac{1}{1 - \left(1 - \frac{wl_2}{b_2}p\right)(1 - t^p)} \left[(\alpha_{t^p} + b_1\beta_{t^p}u)h(u) - (d_2 - \delta t^p)z\right]K_1$$

(9.18)

Having in mind (3.20), it is easy to compute the total wages paid by firms in the capital goods sector

$$W_2 = \frac{\frac{wl_2}{b_2}p}{1 - \left(1 - \frac{wl_2}{b_2}p\right)(1 - t^p)} \left[(\alpha_{t^p} + b_1\beta_{t^p}u)h(u) - (d_2 - \delta t^p)z\right]K_1.$$

(9.19)

We have already stressed that formulas (9.18) and (9.19) hold when $I_1 > d_2K_2$; this condition is satisfied if and only if:

$$z < \frac{\alpha_{t^p} + b_1\beta_{t^p}u}{d_2 - \delta t^p}h(u).$$

(9.20)

9.3.2 Profitability conditions

Firms in the capital goods sector are able to distribute profits in the scheduled measure (3.22) if and only if $I_2 > 0$; this may be viewed as an upper bound of the relative capitalization

$$z < (1 - t^p)\left(1 - \frac{wl_2}{b_2}p\right)\frac{\alpha_{t^p} + b_1\beta_{t^p}u}{d_2 - \delta t^p}h(u).$$

(9.21)

Thus the size of the capital goods sector relative to the other sector has an upper bound (9.21) over which the disproportion jeopardize its profitability.

It is to be stressed that a growing profit tax rate may undermine the profitability of the capital goods sector: since it is plausible that $d_2 > \delta$ the right hand side of (9.21) is decreasing with respect to the tax rate t^p in the interval $[0, 1]$ and is null for $t^p = 1$. Obviously (9.21) implies (9.20), moreover it ensures that profits in the first sector are positive.

9.3.3 Rationing

We conclude this section writing a necessary and sufficient condition for the equilibrium in the capital goods market: output of capital goods is enough to avoid rationing if $b_2K_2 \geqslant I_1^a + I_2$; in terms of relative capitalization this condition reads

$$z \geq \frac{\alpha_{t^p} + b_1\beta_{t^p}u}{b_2\left[1 - \left(1 - \frac{wl_2}{b_2}p\right)(1 - t^p)\right] + d_2 - \delta t^p}h(u).$$

(9.22)

It is worth remarking that the right hand side of (9.22) is less than the right hand side of (4.22); thus the introduction of the profit tax makes the occurrence of rationing less probable..

Hence, in order that (9.21) and (9.22) might hold together it is required that:

$$p \le \frac{b_2\left(1 - t^p\right) - \left(d_2 - \delta t^p\right)}{wl_2\left(1 - t^p\right)}. \tag{9.23}$$

The preceding inequality can be interpreted as an upper bound on the nominal wage pw depending on technical production coefficients of the system b_2, l_2, δ, d_2, and the profit tax rate t^p, just like condition (3.26). However condition (9.23) may also be see as an upper bound on the profit tax rate, depending on technical coefficients and the prevailing real wage rate

$$t^p \le \frac{b_2 - wl_2 p - d_2}{b_2 - wl_2 p - \delta}. \tag{9.24}$$

In particular (9.24) shows the trade off between the profit tax rate t^p and the remuneration rate d_2 of the second sector.

9.4   Dual income tax

It may be interesting to briefly discuss the differences between the case of profit tax treated so far and the case of dual income tax; we devote this section 9.4 to the introduction of a dual income tax (DIT) in our model an to sketch the main characteristic features, contrasting this and the previous case.

9.4.1   Two different tax rates

We assume that the profit tax rate depends on the destination of profits: profits destined to consumption are taxed at a higher rate than those retained for investment. WeWe denote the two rates by $t^{p,1}$ and $t^{p,2}$ respectively (with $t^{p,1} > t^{p,2}$).

The revenue of the DIT is (see also (9.3))

$$T^{dit} = t^{p,1}\left(\Pi_1^c + \Pi_2^c\right) + t^{p,2}\left(\Pi_1^a + \Pi_2^a\right). \tag{9.25}$$

The accumulated profit in sector i, net to the DIT, is (see (9.1))

$$\Pi_i^{a,n} = \left(1 - t^{p,2}\right)\Pi_i^a. \tag{9.26}$$

If d_i is the remuneration rate required by capitalists to invest in firms of sector i when there is no tax, after the introduction of the DIT the (before tax) remuneration rate must rise to[2]

$$d_i^{dit} = \frac{d_i}{1 - t^{p,1}} \; , \qquad (9.27)$$

thus guaranteeing the same net rate as before.

Therefore the before tax consumed part of profit in sector i is

$$\Pi_i^c = d_i^{dit} K_i p_2 \; , \qquad (9.28)$$

while net of tax is (see (9.27) and (9.28))

$$\Pi_i^{c,n} = \left(1 - t^{p,1}\right) \Pi_i^c = d_i K_i p_2 \; . \qquad (9.29)$$

On the other hand the before tax accumulated profit is again given by (3.11) and (3.23), having in mind (9.28), while net of tax it is

$$\Pi_i^{a,n} = \left(1 - t^{p,2}\right) \Pi_i^a \qquad (9.30)$$

9.4.2   The consumption goods sector

We briefly describe the effects of the DIT on the consumption goods sector: the most relevant one is obviously on the dynamics of investment. By (3.10) and (9.30) it is easy to see that the reinvested profit is now given by

$$\Pi_1^{a,n} = \left[\left(1 - t^{p,2}\right)\left(1 - \frac{wl_1}{b_1}\right) pb_1 u - \delta - d_1^{dit}\right] K_1 \qquad (9.31)$$

Formulae (3.18) and (9.31) yield the ex ante investment in the consumption goods sector (see (9.11), (9.9), and (9.10))

$$I_1^a = \max\left\{\left(\alpha^{dit} + b_1 \beta^{dit} u\right) h(u) K_1, 0\right\} \qquad (9.32)$$

where

$$\alpha^{dit} = \delta - \frac{\left(1 - t^{p,2}\right)\delta + \dfrac{1 - t^{p,2}}{1 - t^{p,1}} d_1}{k} \qquad (9.33)$$

and

$$\beta^{dit} = \frac{1 - t^{p,2}}{k}\left(1 - \frac{wl_1}{b_1}\right) p \qquad (9.34)$$

If the consumption goods sector generate enough profit to guarantee its normal capital remuneration rate (9.28), its growth rate is

$$\rho^{dit} = \left(\alpha^{dit} + b_1 \beta^{dit} u\right) h(u) - \delta \qquad (9.35)$$

---

[2] This assumption is the analogous of (9.2)

It may be of some interest to compare the growth rate in this case (DIT) and in the previous one (unique tax rate). It is easy to see that turning to the DIT has a positive impact on the economic growth (i.e. $\rho^{dit} > \rho_{t^p}$), provided that

$$\frac{1 - t^{p,2}}{1 - t^p} > \frac{\delta + \dfrac{d_1}{1 - t^p} + (b_1 - wl_1)\, pu}{\delta + \dfrac{d_1}{1 - t^{p,1}} + (b_1 - wl_1)\, pu} \tag{9.36}$$

If the tax rate on the consumed part of profit does not vary when the DIT is introduced $\left(t^{p,1} = t^p\right)$, then (9.36) simply means $t^{p,2} < t^p$. It is not surprising that a reduction of the tax rate on the accumulated part of profit speeds up economic growth; it is also clear that such reduction causes a fall in the tax income (compare (9.3) and (9.25)).

9.4.3   The capital goods sector

In the preceding subsection we have seen the effects of the DIT on profit and investment in the consumption goods sector, here we pass to calculate the same quantities in the capital goods sector. From (3.21), (9.2), (9.26) and (9.27) we obtain the reinvested part of profit in the capital goods sector as a function of total output Y_2

$$\Pi_2^n = \left(1 - t^{p,2}\right)\left(1 - \frac{wl_2}{b_2}p\right)Y_2 - \left(1 - t^{p,2}\right)\left(d_2^{dit} + \delta\right)K_2 . \tag{9.37}$$

while (4.15) and (14.17) give the investment

$$I_2 = \left(1 - t^{p,2}\right)\left(1 - \frac{wl_2}{b_2}p\right)Y_2 - \left(\frac{1 - t^{p,2}}{1 - t^{p,1}}d_2 - t^{p,2}\delta\right)K_2 . \tag{9.38}$$

Combining (4.15) and (9.38) we obtain output and investment in the capital goods sector (see also the analogous formulae in the other cases (4.16), (4.17), (9.18), (9.19)) when the sector generates enough profit to distribute the scheduled dividends (9.27) (9.28)

$$Y_2 = \frac{1}{1 - \left(1 - t^{p,2}\right)\left(1 - \dfrac{wl_2}{b_2}p\right)}\left[\left(\alpha^{dit} + b_1\beta^{dit}u\right)h\left(u\right) - \left(\frac{1 - t^{p,2}}{1 - t^{p,1}}d_2 - \delta t^{p,2}\right)z\right]$$

$$\tag{9.39}$$

$$I_2 = \frac{\left(1 - t^{p,2}\right)\left(1 - \dfrac{wl_2}{b_2}p\right)\left(\alpha^{dit} + b_1\beta^{dit}u\right)h\left(u\right) - \left(\dfrac{1 - t^{p,2}}{1 - t^{p,1}}d_2 - t^{p,2}\delta\right)z}{1 - \left(1 - t^{p,2}\right)\left(1 - \dfrac{wl_2}{b_2}p\right)}$$

$$\tag{9.40}$$

9.4.4 Normal conditions

We are in position to write the conditions under which both sectors are profitable and there is no rationing of capital goods; just as before[3], if this is the case we say that the system develops under normal conditions.

The profitability condition reads

$$z < \frac{\left(1 - t^{p,2}\right)\left(1 - \dfrac{wl_2}{b_2}p\right)\left(\alpha^{dit} + b_1\beta^{dit}u\right)h(u)}{d_2 - \dfrac{1 - t^{p,1}}{1 - t^{p,2}}t^{p,2}\delta} \tag{9.41}$$

The condition excluding rationing of the capital goods is

$$z > \frac{\left(\alpha^{dit} + b_1\beta^{dit}u\right)h(u)}{b_2\left[1 - (1 - t^{p,2})\left(1 - \dfrac{wl_2}{b_2}p\right)\right] + \dfrac{1 - t^{p,2}}{1 - t^{p,1}}d_2 - t^{p,2}\delta} \tag{9.42}$$

Also in this case it is essential that (9.41) and (9.42) hold together; this is possible provided that

$$t^{p,1} < \frac{b_2 - wl_2p - d_2 - \dfrac{t^{p,2}}{1 - t^{p,2}}\delta}{b_2 - wl_2p - \dfrac{t^{p,2}}{1 - t^{p,2}}\delta} \tag{9.43}$$

Even if it is non clear whether conditions (9.41) and (9.42) are more or less binding that the corresponding inequalities (9.21) and (9.22), valid in the case of a profit tax, it is easy to see that the right hand side of (15.5) is positive only if

$$t^{p,2} < \frac{b_2 - wl_2p - d_2}{b_2 - wl_2p - d_2 + \delta}\,, \tag{9.44}$$

increases as $t^{p,2} \longrightarrow 0$, and in the limit remains below the right hand side of (9.24). Hence the lower is the tax rate on reinvested profit, the easier is for the system to develop under normal conditions, but the constraints on the two rates (9.43) (9.44) are more stringent than in the case of a profit tax (see 9.24 again).

---

[3] See subsections 3.1.2, 4.1.3, 9.3.2, 9.3.3.

10 Balancing the Budget: Equilibria and Stability

In this chapter we analyze the evolution of the economic system when government fiscal policy pursues budget balance. In particular we look for equilibrium points when balancing is obtained either by consumption taxes or through profit taxes or through both of them. In the last sections 10.1.4, 10.2, and 10.3 we address the issues of the stability of the equilibria and the evolution of the system near equilibrium points.

10.1 Evolution of the main variables

As we have seen in the preceding chapter, the fiscal policy affects neither the evolution (3.16) of the capacity utilization rate u, nor the evolution (3.8) (3.30) of the prices p_1 and p_2. Aim of this section is to determine the evolution of the relative capitalization z, and that of the inventory level s, assuming that there is no rationing (9.22) and both sectors are profitable enough (9.21) in order to pay normal dividends (see again (3.12) and (3.22)).

10.1.1 Evolutions of the capital stocks

We begin writing equations for the relative capitalization: we first substitute (9.11) into (3.3) and obtain the evolution of the capital stock in the consumption goods sector

$$\dot{K_1} = -\delta K_1 + (\alpha_{t^P} + b_1 \beta_{t^P} u) h(u) K_1; \tag{10.1}$$

then substitute (9.11) again into (3.3) and obtain the evolution of the capital stock in the capital goods sector

$$\dot{K_2} = -\delta K_2 + \tag{10.2}$$

$$\frac{\left(1 - \frac{wl_2}{b_2}p\right)(1 - t^p)}{1 - \left(1 - \frac{wl_2}{b_2}p\right)(1 - t^p)} \left[(\alpha_{t^p} + b_1\beta_{t^p}u)\,h\,(u) - (d_2 - \delta t^p)\,z\right] K_1.$$

Finally we insert (10.1) and (10.2) into

$$\dot{z} = \frac{\dot{K_2}}{K_1} - z\frac{\dot{K_1}}{K_1} \tag{10.3}$$

and get

$$\dot{z} = H\,(u, s, p, z)\,, \tag{10.4}$$

where

$$H\,(u, s, p, z) = \frac{\left(1 - \frac{wl_2}{b_2}p\right)(1 - t^p)}{1 - \left(1 - \frac{wl_2}{b_2}p\right)(1 - t^p)} \left(\alpha_{t^p} + b_1\beta_{t^p}u\right)h\,(u) - \tag{10.5}$$

$$\left(\frac{(d_2 - \delta t^p)}{1 - \left(1 - \frac{wl_2}{b_2}p\right)(1 - t^p)} + \left(\alpha_{t^p} + b_1\beta_{t^p}u\right)h\,(u)\right)z.$$

10.1.2   Evolution of the inventories

Now we pass to determine the evolution of the inventory level s.

Since the increase of the inventory level is determined by an excess supply of consumption goods, we first have to determine the demand for consumption goods. This is easily obtained substituting (3.4), (9.19), (3.12), and (3.22) into (9.6), having in mind (9.4),

$$D_1 = wl_1upK_1\,(1 - t^c) + \tag{10.6}$$

$$\frac{\frac{wl_2}{b_2}(1 - t^c)}{1 - \left(1 - \frac{wl_2}{b_2}p\right)(1 - t^p)} \left[(\alpha_{t^p} + b_1\beta_{t^p}u)\,h\,(u) - (d_2 - \delta t^p)\,z\right] K_1 +$$

$$\frac{1}{p}\,(d_2K_2 + d_1K_1)\,(1 - t^c) + \frac{1}{p}\,(B + P)\,(1 - t^c).$$

Remark 16 *In the alternative assumption (9.5) that government expenditures on goods and services are free of consumption tax, the last term in the right hand side of (10.6) becomes $\frac{1}{p}\,((1 - t^c)\,B + P)$.*

Under the assumptions of section 9.2, the differential equation yielding the evolution of the inventory level s may be easily obtained from (3.15), (3.7), (3.17), (3.9) and (3.3)

$$\dot{s} = \frac{Y_1 - D_1}{b_1 K_1} - s\frac{I_1 - \delta K_1}{K_1}. \tag{10.7}$$

Substituting (3.1), (10.6), and (9.11) into (10.7), after obvious simplifications, we obtain

$$\dot{s} = G\left(u, s, p, z, K_1, P, B\right), \tag{10.8}$$

where

$$G\left(u, s, p, z, K_1, P, B\right) = \tag{10.9}$$

$$\left(1 - (1 - t^c)\frac{wl_1}{b_1}\right) u -$$

$$\frac{1}{b_1 p}\left(\frac{\frac{wl_2}{b_2}p\left(1 - t^c\right)}{1 - \left(1 - \frac{wl_2}{b_2}p\right)\left(1 - t^p\right)}\right.$$

$$\left. \left[(\alpha_{t^p} + b_1\beta_{t^p}u)\, h\left(u\right) - (d_2 - \delta t^p)\, z\right]\right) +$$

$$\frac{1 - t^c}{b_1 p}\left(d_2 z + d_1\right) + \frac{1 - t^c}{b_1 p}\frac{P + B}{K_1} -$$

$$s\left(\alpha_{t^p} + b_1\beta_{t^p}u\right) h\left(u\right) + s\delta.$$

10.1.3 Equilibria with budget balance

Equations (10.8) and (10.9) shows that the evolution of the inventory level depends crucially on the expenses on consumer goods and direct transfers of the government: in fact it depends on the ratio $\frac{\frac{P+B}{p}(1-t^c)}{b_1 K_1}$ of the demand flow generated by those expenses to the productive capacity of the consumption goods sector. In order to close the model we must specify the fiscal policy; in the present context this means that we must introduce a relation between government expenses $P + B$ and tax revenue $T^c + T^p$.

In this subsection we examine the case of a fiscal policy pursuing budget balance at every time. This amounts to assume that

$$P + B = T^c + T^p. \tag{10.10}$$

Taking account of (9.4) and (9.1), condition (10.10) yields

$$P + B = \frac{t^c}{(1 - t^c)}\left(W_1 + W_2 + \Pi_1^c + \Pi_2^c\right) + \frac{t^p}{(1 - t^c)}\left(\Pi_1 + \Pi_2\right). \tag{10.11}$$

Remark 17 *In the case of Remark 16 (10.11) must be replaced by*

$$P + (1 - t^c) B = t^c (W_1 + W_2 + \Pi_1^c + \Pi_2^c) + t^p (\Pi_1 + \Pi_2). \qquad (10.12)$$

It is clear that this does not change the evolution of the inventory level (10.13)

Substituting (10.11) into (10.9), we obtain the evolution[1] of the inventory level (10.8) in terms of the four variables u, s, p, and z

$$G(u,s,p,z) = \frac{1}{b_1 p} \left[b_1 u p - w l_1 u p - \frac{\frac{w l_2}{b_2} p}{1 - \left(1 - \frac{w l_2}{b_2} p\right)(1 - t^p)} \right.$$

$$[(\alpha_{t^p} + b_1 \beta_{t^p} u) h(u) - (d_2 - \delta t^p) z] -$$

$$\left. (d_2 z + d_1)(1 - t^p) - s b_1 p (\alpha_{t^p} + b_1 \beta_{t^p} u) h(u) + s b_1 p \delta \right].$$

Thus, when both sectors are profitable, there is no rationing, and government balances its budget at every time, the evolution of the economic system may be fully described by a four dimensional system of non-linear ordinary differential equations in the state variables u, s, p and z:

$$\begin{cases} \dot{u} &= F(u,s) \\ \dot{s} &= G(u,s,p,z) \\ \dot{p} &= g_1(s) p \\ \dot{z} &= H(u,s,p,z) \end{cases}. \qquad (10.14)$$

This is the analogous of the dynamical system under normal conditions (4.29).

We deduce equilibrium conditions starting from the third equation in (10.14): obviously $\dot{p} = 0$ if and only if $s = \bar{s}$. If this is the case, then $\dot{u} = 0$ if and only if $u = \bar{u}$. Passing now to the fourth equation in (10.14) we obtain a condition on the relative capitalization z in order to guarantee $\dot{z} = 0$

$$z = \frac{\left(1 - \widehat{V}\right)(\alpha_{t^p} + b_1 \beta_{t^p} u) h(u)}{(d_2 - \delta t^p) + \widehat{V}(\alpha_{t^p} + b_1 \beta_{t^p} u) h(u)}, \qquad (10.15)$$

where

$$\widehat{V} = 1 - \left(1 - \frac{w l_2}{b_2} p\right)(1 - t^p). \qquad (10.16)$$

---

[1] Function G depends on s also via α, β and κ.

Finally $\dot{s} = 0$ if and only if $G(u, s, p, z) = 0$; where $u = \bar{u}$, $s = \bar{s}$, and z is given by (10.15) and (10.16); this means

$$0 = \overline{\overline{k}}\left(\overline{\overline{\alpha}}_{t^p} + b_1\overline{\overline{\beta}}_{t^p}\bar{u}\right) - \left(\frac{\frac{wl_2}{b_2}p}{\widehat{V}} + sb_1 p\right)\left(\overline{\overline{\alpha}}_{t^p} + b_1\overline{\overline{\beta}}_{t^p}\bar{u}\right) + \quad (10.17)$$

$$d_1 t^p + \left[\frac{\frac{wl_2}{b_2}p}{\widehat{V}}(d_2 - \delta t^p) - d_2(1 - t^p)\right]\frac{\left(1 - \widehat{V}\right)\left(\overline{\overline{\alpha}}_{t^p} + b_1\overline{\overline{\beta}}_{t^p}\bar{u}\right)}{(d_2 - \delta t^p) + \widehat{V}\left(\overline{\overline{\alpha}}_{t^p} + b_1\overline{\overline{\beta}}_{t^p}\bar{u}\right)},$$

where $\overline{\overline{k}}$, $\overline{\overline{\alpha}}_{t^p}$, and $\overline{\overline{\beta}}_{t^p}$ are given by (4.5), (9.9), and (9.10) respectively, with $u = \bar{u}$ and $s = \bar{s}$ (see also (12.15), (12.16), (12.17)). Equation (10.17) is to be understood as a condition on the relative price p to obtain equilibrium.

10.1.4 Existence and stability of equilibria

We now come to the existence of equilibrium points for the dynamical system (10.14) under examination. In the following theorem we show that, for a wide range of reasonable tax rates t^p and t^c, the system actually has an equilibrium.

Theorem 6 *For every choice of the consumption tax rate $t^c \in [0, 1]$, if the profit tax rate t^p is sufficiently small, equation (10.17) has at least a solution $\bar{p}$. Thus the differential system (10.14) has at least an equilibrium point $(\bar{u}, \bar{s}, \bar{p}, \bar{z})$, where $\bar{z}$ is the solution of equation (10.15) when $u = \bar{u}$, $s = \bar{s}$, and $p = \bar{p}$. All these equilibria are unstable[2].*

Under the assumptions that there is no profit tax and that the government balances the budget, the dynamical system (10.14) coincides with the dynamical system under normal conditions (4.29), thus the proof of the theorem is again given in the appendix 19.3; the result for small t^p follows trivially.

---

[2] In the present conetxt it is not relevat whether the equilibria are unstable or locally stable with small attraction basin; the crucial difference is between these cases and the existence of a globally attracive equilibrium, since in this case a surely successfull stabilizing policy is simply to do nothing at all and waiting for the sysem to settle down to equilibrium by itself.

10.2 Local dynamics

We get information about the dynamics around the equilibrium point examining what happens when $t^p = 0$. In this case equation (10.17) is an identity, the system (10.14) has infinitely many equilibrium points and the Jacobian matrix has a null eigenvalue at each such point (see appendix 19.10). Since the existence of a zero eigenvalue[3] makes the use of the linear approximation to perform the analysis not possible, we use the adiabatic principle[4].

10.2.1 Adiabatic approximation

For this purpose it is necessary to diagonalize the Jacobian matrix J of the dynamical system; we introduce, therefore, the matrix $\widehat{B} = (v_1, v_2, v_3, v_4)$, with v_i $(i = 1, \ldots, 4)$ representing the eigenvectors of the Jacobian matrix. Therefore $\widehat{B}^{-1} J \widehat{B} = diag(\lambda_i)$ $(i = 1, \ldots, 4)$. Let us introduce the new variables[5] x_i $(i = 1, \ldots, 4)$.

In the new coordinate system the axes x_1 and x_4 are the two eigenspaces corresponding to the negative eigenvalues; hence by the adiabatic principle we may approximate the solution of the dynamical system by setting $\dot{x}_1 = \dot{x}_4 = 0$. Obvious simplifications allow us to write:

$$0 = F(u, s) + \frac{\partial F(\bar{u}, \bar{s})}{\partial s} \frac{G(u, s, p)}{\lambda_1} \tag{10.18}$$

$$z = -\frac{\partial H(\bar{\eta})}{\partial p} \frac{1}{H_1(\bar{\eta})} \frac{g(s)p}{H_1(\eta)} + \frac{H_2(\eta)}{H_1(\eta)}, \tag{10.19}$$

where the following notation has been used:

$$H_1(\eta) = (\alpha_{t^p} + b_1 \beta_{t^p} u) h(u) + \frac{d_2 b_2}{w l_2 p} \tag{10.20}$$

$$H_2(\eta) = \frac{b_2 - w l_2 p}{w l_2 p} (\alpha_{t^p} + b_1 \beta_{t^p} u) h(u), \tag{10.21}$$

with $H(\eta) = H_1(\eta) z + H_2(\eta)$ and where $\eta = (u, s, p, z)$.

Clearly equation (10.8) describes the evolution of the relative price p when the evolution of the rate of capacity utilization u and of the ratio of inventories s are known; equations (10.4) and (10.5) yield the evolution of the relative fixed capital stock. Further details may again be found in the appendix 19.10.

---

[3] As in the preceding case a zero eigenvalue makes the equilibria not hyperbolic; it is not possible therefore to use the Hartman-Grobman theorem.

[4] We again refer the reader to [45] and [90] for an exposition of this method of analysis.

[5] Again these variables are analogous to the principal coordinates of [37]; we refer the reader to the mathematical appendix for the explicit expression of the transformation.

10.3   Expansion and depression

Also in this case the system may evolve towards two different regimes.

10.3.1   Expansion

The first regime is characterized by a falling ratio of inventories and an increasing rate of capacity utilization; if the bounds (9.21), (9.22) and (9.23) were not binding there would be a $t = \tilde{t}$ such that:

$$
\begin{cases}
\lim_{t \to \tilde{t}^-} p(t) & = & +\infty \\
\lim_{t \to \tilde{t}^-} s(t) & = & 0 \\
\lim_{t \to \tilde{t}^-} u(t) & = & \tilde{u}
\end{cases}
\tag{10.22}
$$

where $\bar{u} < \tilde{u} < 1$. The assumption that $\lim_{s \to 0^+} sg_1(s) = +\infty$ together with:

$$
\lim_{t \to \tilde{t}^-} G(u, s, p) = \left(1 - \frac{wl_1}{b_1} \right) (1 - h(\tilde{u})) \in \mathbb{R}_+
\tag{10.23}
$$

yields:

$$
\lim_{t \to \tilde{t}^-} s(t) p(t) = +\infty.
\tag{10.24}
$$

As we have already seen this regimes leads to an eventual overheating of the economy (see section 6.2.1).

10.3.2   Depression

The second type of asymptotic behavior of the solutions of the dynamical system (10.14) takes place when the inventory level is ever rising while the capacity utilization rate is falling. Also in this case, if the bounds (9.21), (9.22) and (9.23) were not binding, it is easy to show that there would exist a time $\hat{t}$ such that:

$$
\begin{cases}
\lim_{t \to \hat{t}^-} p(t) & = & 0 \\
\lim_{t \to \hat{t}^-} s(t) & = & +\infty \\
\lim_{t \to \hat{t}^-} u(t) & = & \hat{u}
\end{cases}
\tag{10.25}
$$

where $0 < \hat{u} < \bar{u}$. In this case too the condition $\lim_{s \to +\infty} sg_1(s) = -\infty$ yields:

$$
\lim_{t \to \hat{t}^-} s(t) p(t) = 0.
\tag{10.26}
$$

We call this alternative behavior the depression regime.

Thus, when the equilibrium is lost, the evolution of the system is two fold. It may enter either a depression regime with declining demand and falling investment or an accelerated develope with rapidly increasing demand in both sectors; in this case excess demand eventually arises in both sectors that causes price increases and eventually result in an overheating phase.

10.3.3   Stabilizing strategies and government budget

In the two following chapters 11 and 12 we examine some strategies directed towards the stabilization of the equilibrium point(s).

Here we do not assume that the government is constrained to maintain budget balance at every time, as in subsection 10.1.3. The government can finance extraordinary interventions by deficit spending; this is possible for sure if the (foreign) demand for government bonds is perfectly elastic: we assume that this is the case. Conversely the government can also increase the budget surplus either issuing new taxes or rising current tax rates, while expenses remain unchanged.

This assumption is acceptable only if these interventions are temporary and this is really the case if they are able to drive the system towards an equilibrium, so that their size is decreasing in time and they can be revoked after some time.

If we are able to prove that convergence takes actually place, this assumption simply means that the outstanding debt is never expected to explode, since the rise in government spending, necessary to overcome a slump, may be compensated after some time by a budget surplus, generated by an increase of taxes necessary to control inflation during the subsequent recovery phase.

All the preceding arguments would become irrelevant if we were examining the system far from equilibrium; in this case these strategies would cause a permanent and systematic budget unbalance, which would become infeasible in the long run. For this reason we have not described the dynamical systems describing the reaction of the economy to government interventions far from normal equilibria.

11 Anti-inflationary Policies

This chapter is devoted to the analysis the effectiveness of some anti-inflationary fiscal policies. Since an increase of the price of consumption goods is caused by a demand exceeding current production and depleting the stocks, a possible strategy aimed to reduce inflation may be a fiscal policy that reduces the increase of the demand.

We are going to examine two different policies aimed to cool the demand down: an increase of the consumption tax rate and an increase of the profit tax rate. Both of them may be implemented in two different ways: the first one consists in fixing a target for the price of consumption goods and trying to drive the system towards that target, while the second one consists in trying to stabilize the consumer price index.

11.1 Effects of a rise of the consumption tax rate

During the overheating phase the price of consumption goods rises at rate $g_1(s)$ (see (3.8) and (10.22)): hence in our model $g_1(s)$ may be viewed as the inflation rate measured in terms of the consumer price index.

We assume that, when the price p_1 of consumption goods rises, the government steps in increasing the consumption tax rate t^c. There are many different ways to do this and the choice depends obviously on the macroeconomic targets of the fiscal policy. We analyze two alternative strategies: the first one is in some sense more ambitious since it aims at stabilizing prices at a target level (see subsection 11.1.1); the second one simply pursues the progressive reduction of the inflation rate (see subsection 11.1.2).

11.1.1   Stabilizing the general price level

In order to drive the system to the desired price level[1] $\bar{p}_1$ we assume that the increase of the consumption tax rate t^c is larger the larger is the gap $p_1 - \bar{p}_1$ between the actual and the desired price levels

$$t^c = \bar{t}^c + \vartheta(p_1), \tag{11.1}$$

where $\bar{t}^c$ is the rate assuring the budget balance (see (10.14) and (10.10)) and $\vartheta \in C^{(1)}$ is a strictly increasing function such that $\vartheta(\bar{p}_1) = 0$.

Government budget

We begin our analysis assuming that there is no profit tax (i.e. $t^p = 0$), thus (10.14) and (10.10) become

$$P + B = \bar{t}^c \left(W_1 + W_2 + \Pi_1^c + \Pi_2^c + P + B \right) \tag{11.2}$$

and

$$P + B = \frac{\bar{t}^c}{1 - \bar{t}^c} \left(W_1 + W_2 + \Pi_1^c + \Pi_2^c \right) \tag{11.3}$$

respectively.

We also assume an early intervention, in the sense that government intervenes before either rationing takes place or one of the two sectors begins loosing its profitability. Analyticaly this means so that both (9.21) and (9.22) hold throughout our analysis.

Demand for consumption goods

Substituting (11.3) into (10.6) we obtain the demand for consumption goods after the increase of the consumption tax rate

$$D_1 = \left(1 - \frac{\vartheta(p_1)}{1 - \bar{t}^c} \right) \frac{W_1 + W_2 + \Pi_1^c + \Pi_2^c}{p_1}. \tag{11.4}$$

The evolution of the inventory level is again given by (10.8); however the function $G(u, s, p, z)$ now is obtained substituting in (10.9) the right hand side of (11.3) instead of (10.10), taking (11.4) into account. Thus the

---

[1]We remember that near the normal equilibria the price of the capital goods p_2 is stationary. Thus the stabilization of the consumption goods price p_1 is sufficient for the stabilization of the general price level.

evolution of the inventory level turns out to be independent of the relative capitalization z and the function G has the form

$$G(u,s,p) = \frac{k}{b_1 p}(\alpha + b_1\beta u)(1 - h(u)) + \tag{11.5}$$

$$\frac{\vartheta(p_1)}{1 - \bar{t}^c}\frac{1}{b_1 p}(wl_1 pu + (\alpha + b_1\beta u)h(u) + d_1).$$

Differential system

The dynamical system (10.14) is now replaced by

$$\begin{cases} \dot{u} &= F(u,s) \\ \dot{s} &= G(u,s,p) \\ \dot{p} &= g_1(s)p \\ \dot{z} &= H(u,s,p,z) \end{cases}, \tag{11.6}$$

where the function $G(u,s,p)$ is given by (11.5), while the function $H(u,s,p,z)$ is given by

$$H(u,s,p,z) = (\alpha + b_1\beta u)h(u) - \left(\frac{d_2}{\frac{wl_2}{b_2}p} + (\alpha + b_1\beta u)h(u)\right)z, \tag{11.7}$$

which is precisely (10.5) with $t^p = 0$.

Equilibria

Theorem 7 *The differential system (11.6) has a unique equilibrium point $(\bar{u},\bar{s},\bar{p},\bar{z})$ where $\bar{u}$ and $\bar{s}$ are the normal values of the capacity utilization rate and of the level of inventories respectively.*

$$\bar{p} = \frac{\bar{p}_1}{p_2} \tag{11.8}$$

and the relative stock of capital $\bar{z}$ satisfies

$$\bar{z} = \frac{b_2 - wl_2\bar{p}}{wl_2\bar{p}}\frac{\bar{\alpha} + b_1\bar{\beta}\bar{u}}{(\bar{\alpha} + b_1\bar{\beta}\bar{u}) + \frac{d_2 b_2}{wl_2\bar{p}}}, \tag{11.9}$$

with $\bar{\alpha}$ and $\bar{\beta}$ evaluated at $\bar{p}$ and $\bar{k} = 1 + b_1\bar{s}\bar{p}$.
If

$$\vartheta'(\bar{p}_1) > \frac{\dfrac{\partial F(\bar{\eta})}{\partial s}}{g_1'(\bar{s})}\frac{h'(\bar{u})}{\dfrac{\overline{p_2}}{1 - \bar{t}^c}}\frac{\bar{k}(\bar{\alpha} + b_1\bar{\beta}\bar{u})}{(wl_1\overline{pu} + (\bar{\alpha} + b_1\bar{\beta}\bar{u}) + d_1)} \tag{11.10}$$

then the equilibrium point (11.8), (11.9) is locally attractive.

The proof is sketched in the appendix 19.11.

Having in mind theorem 6, it is easy to extend the above result to the case of a small (positive) profit tax rate.

Corollary 8 *If the profit tax rate t^p is positive and sufficiently small, then the equilibrium point (11.8) (11.9) is still stable provided that $\bar{p}$ is sufficiently larger than the right hand side of (11.10). Obviously in this case equations (11.5) and (11.7) must be replaced by (10.9) and (10.5) respectively.*

Remark 18 *Condition (11.10) is certainly satisfied if the capital goods price level $\bar{p}_2$ is not too low.*

The condition is more binding the larger the reaction to production disequilibrium (i.e. $h'(\bar{u})$) of firms in the consumption goods sector is. On the other hand a stronger increase of the consumption tax rate (i.e. an increase of $\theta'(\bar{p}_1)$) weakens the condition.

The reaction of firms to stock disequilibrium plays a more ambiguous role since it affects both prices (via $g'(\bar{s})$) and quantities (via $\dfrac{\overline{\partial F}}{\partial s}$); it is apparent that a stronger price reaction makes stability easier, whereas a stronger quantity reaction has an opposite outcome. Such a result is natural if we notice that a quantity reaction requires an increase of employment and investment which have direct and indirect consequences on the demand for consumption goods, while this is not the case for a price reaction.

11.1.2 Diminishing the inflation rate

A strategy aimed at diminishing the inflation rate may be an increase of the consumption tax rate such that the increase is proportional to the rate of growth $g_1(s)$ of the price itself

$$t^c = \overline{t^c} + \vartheta g_1(s), \tag{11.11}$$

where $\overline{t^c}$ is again the rate assuring the budget balance (see (10.14) and (10.10)) and $\vartheta > 0$.

Government budget and demand for consumption goods

In this case we restrict our analysis to the case without profit tax, i.e. $t^p = 0$ and assume that the government intervene when the economy is still in its normal conditions, thus both (9.21) and (9.22) hold.

As in the preceding case, substituting (11.3) into (10.6) we obtain the demand for consumption goods after the increase of the consumption tax rate

$$D_1 = \left(1 - \frac{\vartheta g_1(s)}{1 - \overline{t^c}}\right) \frac{W_1 + W_2 + \Pi_1^c + \Pi_2^c}{p_1}. \tag{11.12}$$

The evolution of the inventory level is again given by (10.8); however the function $G(u, s, p, z)$ now is obtained substituting in (10.9) the right hand side of (11.3) instead of (10.10), taking (11.12) into account. Thus the evolution of the inventory level turns out to be independent of the relative capitalization z and the function G has the form

$$G(u, s, p) = \frac{k}{b_1 p} (\alpha + b_1 \beta u)(1 - h(u)) + \qquad (11.13)$$
$$\frac{\vartheta g_1(s)}{1 - \bar{t}^c} \frac{1}{b_1 p} (w l_1 p u + (\alpha + b_1 \beta u) h(u) + d_1).$$

Differential system

The dynamical system (10.14) is now replaced by

$$\begin{cases} \dot{u} &= F(u, s) \\ \dot{s} &= G(u, s, p) \\ \dot{p} &= g_1(s) p \\ \dot{z} &= H(u, s, p, z) \end{cases}, \qquad (11.14)$$

where the function $G(u, s, p)$ is given by (11.13), while the function $H(u, s, p, z)$ is still given by (11.7).

Equilibria

Theorem 9 *The differential system (11.14) has a one dimensional manifold of equilibrium points; all of them are of the form $(\bar{u}, \bar{s}, \bar{p}, \bar{z})$ where $\bar{u}$ and $\bar{s}$ are the normal values of the capacity utilization rate and of the level of inventories respectively. The equilibrium values for the relative price $\bar{p}$ and for the relative stock of fixed capital $\bar{z}$ satisfy*

$$\bar{z} = \frac{b_2 - w l_2 \bar{p}}{w l_2 \bar{p}} \frac{\bar{\alpha} + b_1 \bar{\beta} \bar{u}}{(\bar{\alpha} + b_1 \bar{\beta} \bar{u}) + \dfrac{d_2 b_2}{w l_2 \bar{p}}}, \qquad (11.15)$$

with $\bar{\alpha}$ and $\bar{\beta}$ evaluated at $\bar{p}$ and $\bar{k} = 1 + b_1 \bar{s} \bar{p}$.
These equilibria are locally stable if and only if

$$\vartheta > (1 - \bar{t}^c) \frac{\overline{\dfrac{\partial F}{\partial s}}}{\overline{\dfrac{\partial F}{\partial u}}} \frac{h'(\bar{u})}{-g_1'(\bar{s})} \frac{\bar{k}(\bar{\alpha} + b_1 \bar{\beta} \bar{u})}{w l_1 \overline{p u} + (\bar{\alpha} + b_1 \bar{\beta} \bar{u}) + d_1}. \qquad (11.16)$$

Where, as before, the upper bar means that the function is calculated in the equilibrium point $(\bar{u}, \bar{s}, \bar{p}, \bar{z})$.

The proof is in the appendix 19.10.

Remark 19 *The stability condition (11.16) is simply a lower bound on the additional consumption tax rate $\vartheta g_1(s)$.*

The stronger is the accelerator (i.e. the larger is $h'(\overline{u})$), the more binding is condition (11.16). On the other hand, the stronger is the reaction of prices to disequilibrium (i.e. the larger is $g'_1(\overline{s})$) and the larger is the equilibrium consumption tax rate t^c, the less binding is condition (11.16). This confirms the intuition that the accelerator has a destabilizing effect, while the reaction of prices to excess demand and the rise of the consumption tax have a stabilizing effect.

11.2   Effects of a rise in the profit tax

A possible alternative to the rise of the consumption tax may be the rise of the profit tax. As in the preceding case 11.1 we discuss two different strategies: the first one links the tax rate to the gap between the actual price level and the target one, the second one links it to the inflation rate.

In both case the intervention takes place before the overheating of the economy, this means that conditions (9.21) and (9.22) hold.

11.2.1   Demand and evolution of the inventories

As first step of our analysis we check the impact of the profit tax on the demand for consumption goods, when the government balances its budget by the consumption tax only; this means that instead of (10.10) we have

$$B + P = T^c. \tag{11.17}$$

While the consumed part of profit of both sectors and the total wages payed by the consumption goods sector do not vary (and are again given by (9.7), (9.14), and (3.4)), the wages payed by the capital goods sector are now given by (9.19); substituting now into (9.6) and taking (11.17) into account, we obtain

$$D_1 = \frac{1}{p}\left[wl_1 pu + \frac{\frac{wl_2}{b_2}p}{1 - \left(1 - \frac{wl_2}{b_2}p\right)(1 - t^p)} \right. $$
$$\left. [(\alpha_{t^p} + b_1\beta_{t^p}u)\,h(u) - (d_2 - \delta t^p)\,z] + d_1 + d_2 z \right] \tag{11.18}$$

It is now easy to obtain the evolution of the inventory level (10.8) where

$$G(u,s,p,z) = \frac{k}{b_1 p}(\alpha_{t^p} + b_1\beta_{t^p}u)(1 - h(u)) + \tag{11.19}$$

$$\frac{t^p}{b_1 p} \left((b_1 - wl_1) \, pu + \frac{1 - \frac{wl_2}{b_2} p}{1 - \left(1 - \frac{wl_2}{b_2} p\right)(1 - t^p)} \cdot \right.$$

$$\left. [(\alpha_{t^p} + b_1 \beta_{t^p} u) \, h(u) - d_2 z] - \frac{\frac{wl_2}{b_2} p}{1 - \left(1 - \frac{wl_2}{b_2} p\right)(1 - t^p)} \delta z \right)$$

11.2.2 Stabilizing the general price level

Government budget

As in the case of section 11.1.1 we assume that the government intervenes when the price of consumption goods p_1 exceeds its target value $\overline{p}_1$.

As in that case we begin assuming that before the intervention the government balances the budget by means of a consumption tax with fixed tax rate $\overline{t}^c$, hence

$$t^c = \overline{t^c} \tag{11.20}$$

(see (10.14) and (10.10)).

Thus the government introduces a profit tax with tax rate increasing as the gap $p_1 - \overline{p}_1$ between the actual and the desired price levels rises

$$t^p = \vartheta(p_1); \tag{11.21}$$

here $\vartheta \in C^{(1)}$ is a strictly increasing function such that $\vartheta(\overline{p}_1) = 0$.

Equilibria

Substituting (11.21) and (11.20) into (11.2) we obtain the evolution of the inventory level in the present case, while the evolution of the relative capitalization is still given by (10.5).

Now we look for the existence of equilibria of the differential system (10.14) in the case under examination.

Theorem 10 *Under the assumptions (11.21), and (11.2), $(\overline{u}, \overline{s}, \overline{p}, \overline{z})$ is an equilibrium point of the system (10.14) ; once again $\overline{u}$ and $\overline{s}$ are the normal values of the capacity utilization rate and of the ratio of inventories to the productive capacity respectively and the equilibrium values for the relative price $\overline{p}$ and for the relative stock of fixed capital $\overline{z}$ satisfy*

$$\overline{p} = \frac{\overline{p}_1}{\overline{p}_2} \tag{11.22}$$

$$H(\overline{u}, \overline{s}, \overline{p}, \overline{z}) = 0. \tag{11.23}$$

This equilibrium is locally stable, provided that the growth rate of the profit tax is sufficiently large (in the sense of (19.57)).

The proof can be found in the appendix 19.12.

Remark 20 *It is worth stressing that on the one hand an increase of the profit tax has a stabilizing effect only if the tax rate is sufficiently high (in the sense of the above theorem 10). On the other hand there is a threshold (9.24) over that the profit tax destroys the equilibria of the economy as it perturbs investment and alters the growth of both sectors.*

We may conclude that in general the introduction (or the increase) of profit taxes is stabilizing only if the economy is very near a normal equilibrium.

Remark 21 *Through the above discussion we have steadily maintained that announcement and implementation of the fiscal policy do not affect the behavior of the agents of the economy. This may be not the case if a rise of the profit tax is first announced and then implemented: in this case it is conceivable that the propensity to invest is negatively affected. In the present context this may be portrayed by a fall in the accelerator $h(u)$ and its steepness. If this is the case the fiscal policy may result more effective, since the stability may be obtained with a less severe profit tax increase. 'In the analysis of the stability of the overall level of activity, the point at issue is not the optimal character of firms behavior, but that of the monetary institutions. Taking the behavior of firms as given, it appears easy to determine an appropriate degree of reaction on the part of monetary institutions (i.e. an appropriate value of its reaction coefficients). If the destabilizing character of the reaction of firms is increased, one must modify the functioning of monetary institutions. Considering the entire dynamic system, it is even possible to define* optimal *reaction coefficients, i.e. those which ensure the fastest convergence.* [2]

11.2.3 Diminishing the inflation

Government budget

As in the preceding cases 11.1.1, 11.1.2, and 11.2.2 we begin our analysis assuming that in equilibrium the government balances its budget by means of the consumption tax only and that its rate is constant over time (see (11.25), having in mind (11.2) and (11.3)).

When the price of consumption goods rises, the government begins levying a profit tax with tax rate t^p proportional to the rate of growth $g_1(s)$ of the price

$$t^p = \vartheta g_1(s), \tag{11.24}$$

with $\vartheta > 0$. (see (11.11)).

---

[2] See Dumenil and Levy (1993) p. 216, the role of institutions.

Equilibria

In the present context (see (10.13) and (11.20)) the function $G(u, s, p, z)$, determining the evolution of the inventory level, takes the form

$$G(u, s, p, z) = \frac{k}{b_1 p} \left(\alpha_{t^p} + b_1 \beta_{t^p} u\right) \left(1 - h(u)\right) + \tag{11.25}$$

$$\frac{\vartheta g_1(s)}{b_1 p} \left[\left(\frac{\left(1 - \frac{wl_2}{b_2} p\right) \left(\alpha_{t^p} + b_1 \beta_{t^p} u\right) h(u) - \delta}{1 - \left(1 - \frac{wl_2}{b_2} p\right) \left(1 - \vartheta g_1(s)\right)} \right) + \right.$$

$$\left. d_1 + \frac{1 + \left(\vartheta g_1(s) - 2\right) \left(1 - \frac{wl_2}{b_2} p\right)}{1 - \left(1 - \frac{wl_2}{b_2} p\right) \left(1 - \vartheta g_1(s)\right)} d_2 z \right].$$

Now we are in position to describe the equilibria of the differential system (10.14) in the case under examination.

Theorem 11 *Under the assumptions (11.16), (11.24), and (11.2), the system (10.14), with G given by (11.25), has a one dimensional manifold of equilibrium points; all of them are of the form $(\bar{u}, \bar{s}, \bar{p}, \bar{z})$ where $\bar{u}$ and $\bar{s}$ are the normal values of the capacity utilization rate and of the ratio of inventories respectively and the equilibrium values for the relative price $\bar{p}$ and for the relative stock of fixed capital $\bar{z}$ satisfy*

$$H(\bar{u}, \bar{s}, \bar{p}, \bar{z}) = 0, \tag{11.26}$$

All these equilibria are stable provided that the profit tax rate ϑ is sufficiently large (see condition (19.65)).

The proof can be found in the appendix 19.13.

Corollary 12 *If the assumption (11.24) is replaced by*

$$t^p = \bar{t}^p + \vartheta g_1(s), \tag{11.27}$$

then, for every positive and sufficiently small $\bar{t}^p$, the system (10.14) has at least one equilibrium point and this point is locally stable provided that the rate of growth of the tax rate t^p is sufficiently large.

Remark 22 *As in the cases discussed in subsections 11.1.1 and 11.1.2, also here and in subsection 11.2.2 the stability conditions on the tax rates are less binding the larger is the price reaction $g'(\bar{s})$, while it is more requiring the lager are the quantity reactions $\dfrac{\partial F(\bar{\eta})}{\partial s}$ and $\bar{h}'$.*

For further comments we refer again to remarks in 11.1.1 and 11.1.2. In particular the warning of remark 20 applies in this case too and the considerations of remark 21.

11.2.4   Some concluding remarks

The analysis performed in this chapter has clearly shown that a consumption tax with variable rate is the most effective anti-inflationary fiscal policy that the government may choose. Moreover, the implementation of such a strategy entails only limited information processing since the government is simply assumed to know the inflation rate measured by the consumer price index[3].

A different strategy consists in levying a profit rate with variable rate, but from the above discussion[4] it is apparent that this alternative is rather limited in scope because of the emergence of two drawbacks. On the one hand the increase of the tax rate can not exceed the upper bound over which the perturbation of the investment strategies of firms in both sectors destroys the normal equilibria of the system[5]. On the other hand a profit tax lowers the equilibrium growth rate of the system[6].

The only reason for preferring this alternative may be its political appeal, since no further advantage seems to outweigh these faults.

One may wonder whether a dual income tax may circumvent these difficulties. An elementary though troublesome calculation shows that a DIT may be designed to lower the inflation choosing suitable tax rates, depending on the consumer price index.

As shown in section 9.4 this may allow to reduce the negative feedback on the growth rate, but at the expense of further reducing the range of the tax rates compatible with the existence of normal equilibria.

---

[3] See subsections 11.1.1 and 11.1.2.

[4] See subsections 11.2.2 and 11.2.3.

[5] As shown in theorem 6.

[6] As shown by formula (9.13).

12 Expansionary Policies

The aim of this chapter is to assess the effectiveness of some expansionary fiscal policies, which may be implemented in order to support production and employment during slumps.

As we have seen, when the economy enters a depression phase, a sluggish demand trend shows up in involuntary accumulation of stocks, decline of production, and a more than proportional fall in investment (see (10.25)); profits and employment decline.

We shall examine two possible strategies to contrast the decline of the demand: tax cuts and setting up of unemployment benefits

12.1 Effects of a tax cut

Reducing taxes during a depression phase is obviously a strategy perfectly symmetric to rising them during an overheating phase: in this sense such policy is the reverse of the anti-inflationary policy discussed in the previous section.

12.1.1 Consumption tax

As in the case of section 11.1, we assume that in equilibrium the government balances its budget by a fixed rate proportional consumption tax. When the involuntary accumulation of stocks begins, the government cuts the consumption tax and that the larger is stock disequilibrium, the larger is the cut.

$$t^c = \bar{t}^c + q(s). \tag{12.1}$$

Here $\bar{t}^c$ is the tax rate assuring the budget balance (10.11), q is a $C^{(1)}$ function with $q(\bar{s}) = 0$ and $q' < 0$.

Also in this case we begin assuming that $t^p = 0$.

It is plain that this case can be treated just reverting the arguments of section 11.1; hence the differential system is again (11.14), where

$$G(u, s, p, z) \;=\; \frac{k}{b_1 p}\,(\alpha + b_1 \beta u)\,(1 - h(u)) + \tag{12.2}$$

$$\frac{q(s)}{1 - \bar{t}^c}\frac{1}{b_1 p}\,(wl_1 up + (\alpha + b_1 \beta u)\,h(u) + d_1)\,,$$

and $H(u, s, p, z)$ is again given by (11.7).

Theorem 13 *The differential system (11.14), with G given by (12.2), has a one dimensional manifold of equilibrium points; all of them are of the form $(\bar{u}, \bar{s}, \bar{p}, \bar{z})$ where $\bar{u}$ and $\bar{s}$ are the normal values of the capacity utilization rate and of the ratio of inventories respectively, while the equilibrium values for the relative price $\bar{p}$ and for the relative stock of fixed capital $\bar{z}$ satisfy*

$$\bar{z} = \frac{b_2 - wl_2\bar{p}}{wl_2\bar{p}}\,\frac{\bar{\alpha} + b_1\bar{\beta}\bar{u}}{(\bar{\alpha} + b_1\bar{\beta}\bar{u}) + \dfrac{d_2 b_2}{wl_2\bar{p}}}\,, \tag{12.3}$$

with $\bar{\alpha}$ and $\bar{\beta}$ evaluated at $\bar{p}$ and $\bar{k} = 1 + b_1\bar{s}\bar{p}$. All these equilibria are locally stable if

$$-q'(\bar{s}) > (1 - \bar{t}^c)\,\frac{\dfrac{\partial F}{\partial s}}{\dfrac{\partial F}{\partial u}}\,\frac{(\bar{\alpha} + b_1\bar{\beta}\bar{u})\,h'(\bar{u})}{wl_1\overline{pu} + (\bar{\alpha} + b_1\bar{\beta}\bar{u}) + d_1}\,. \tag{12.4}$$

The proof is the same of theorem 9 in the appendix 19.10.

Remark 23 *Also this result may be generalized to the case of a government balancing its budget in equilibrium by both consumption and profit taxes, provided that the profit tax rate is not too large (see corollary 8) .*

12.1.2 Profit tax

Also the case of a cut of the profit tax can be treated reverting the arguments of section 11.2. We again denote by $\bar{t}^c$ and $\bar{t}^c$ the fixed tax rates that guarantee the budget balance in equilibrium and assume that the government cuts the profit tax when involuntary stockpiling takes places

$$t^p = \bar{t}^c + q(s), \tag{12.5}$$

where again q is a $C^{(1)}$ function with $q(\bar{s}) = 0$ and $q' < 0$.

This case and that discussed in corollary 12 are perfectly symmetric; hence

$$
\begin{aligned}
G(u, s, p, z) \;=\; & \frac{k}{b_1 p}\left(\alpha_{t^p} + b_1\beta_{t^p}u\right)(1 - h(u)) + && (12.6) \\[2mm]
& \frac{q(s)}{b_1 p}\left[\left(\frac{\left(1 - \frac{wl_2}{b_2}p\right)\left(\alpha_{t^p} + b_1\beta_{t^p}u\right)h(u) - \delta}{1 - \left(1 - \frac{wl_2}{b_2}p\right)(1 - q(s))}\right) + \right. \\[2mm]
& \left. d_1 + \frac{1 + (q(s) - 2)\left(1 - \frac{wl_2}{b_2}p\right)}{1 - \left(1 - \frac{wl_2}{b_2}p\right)(1 - q(s))}d_2 z\right].
\end{aligned}
$$

In analogy with that corollary, we can conclude that the differential system (10.14) with G given by (12.6) has at least an equilibrium point of the form $(\bar{u}, \bar{s}, \bar{p}, \bar{z})$. This point is stable if and only if

$$
-q'(\bar{s}) \;>\; \frac{\dfrac{\partial F(\bar{\eta})}{\partial s}}{\dfrac{\partial F(\bar{\eta})}{\partial u}} \tag{12.7}
$$

$$
\frac{\overline{k}\left(\bar{\alpha} + b_1\bar{\beta}\bar{u}\right)\bar{h}'}{(b_1 - wl_1)\overline{pu} + \dfrac{(b_2 - wl_2\overline{p})\left(\bar{\alpha} + b_1\bar{\beta}\bar{u}\right)}{wl_2\overline{p}\left(\bar{\alpha} + b_1\bar{\beta}\bar{u}\right) + b_2 d_2}\left(\bar{\alpha} + b_1\bar{\beta}\bar{u} - \delta + d_2\right)}.
$$

Remark 24 *Also in this case we underline the possible inconsistency of the above condition (12.7), requiring that the reduction of the profit tax rate is sufficiently high, with the condition that the equilibrium tax rate $\bar{t}^c$ is small and compatible with the profitability conditions in both sectors. This confirms that the strategy relying on profit tax variations is effective only on a possibly very small neighborhood of the equilibrium.*

This is an added argument[1] in favor of an intervention on the consumption tax instead on the profit tax.

The proof of this result is completely analogous to that of theorem 11 in the appendix 19.13.

---

[1] Beside those discussed in subsection 11.2.4.

12.2 Effects of the introduction of unemployment benefits

By our assumptions on the production technology in both sectors, the total employment is proportional to the total output (see (3.3) and (3.30)); hence also the total wages paid to workers in each sector are directly proportional to the total output.

When the total output declines, the same happens to aggregate wage bill and eventually to the demand for consumption goods. Thus the system enters the depression regime outlined in subsection 5.3.2 and in chapter 6.

A possible policy aimed at contrasting this evolution may be to set up unemployment benefits that guarantee a minimum income to workers loosing their jobs because of the slowing down of the productive activity.

12.2.1   Unemployment measurement

We assume that the government intervene when the employment falls under the equilibrium level in both sectors. The equilibrium employment is the level of employment when the capacity utilization rate and the inventory level are at their normal values, the government balances its budget, and there is no inflation.

As in all preceding cases we begin our analysis assuming that, before the intervention, there is only a consumption tax with fixed tax rate t^c and that its revenue balances the government budget. We assume further that the unemployment benefits, paid to workers loosing their jobs when the production falls below its normal (or equilibrium) level, are financed by deficit spending.

This must not be understood in the sense that the government does not support possible unemployed people when the system is in equilibrium; it simply means that, if in equilibrium there are still workless people, this must be considered as structural unemployment and any income support for them must be viewed as a permanent transfer to households and financed by means of ordinary taxation.

We denote the unemployment connected with the current economic situation and the amount of unemployment benefits paid to these workers by U and B_U respectively, while we denote permanent transfer expenditures of the government by $\overline{B}$. As explained above the latter may include expenses for structural unemployment benefits.

12.2.2   Unemployment benefits

Following our previous assumptions we may write

$$T^c = \overline{B} + P \tag{12.8}$$

and
$$B = \overline{B} + B_U. \tag{12.9}$$

The normal employment levels in the two sectors are $\overline{L_1}$ and $\overline{L_2}$ respectively; they are determined assuming that the capacity utilization rate u and the inventory level s are at their respective normal values $\overline{u}$ and $\overline{s}$, whereas both the prices p_1 and p_2 and the dimensions K_1 and K_2 are those prevailing at the measurement time. This means that the normal employment levels are determined in reference to the current structure of the real productive system and not in reference to an fully balanced ideal one.

Thus we have
$$U = \overline{L_1} - L_1 + \overline{L_2} - L_2, \tag{12.10}$$

where
$$\overline{L_1} = l_1 \overline{u} K_1 \tag{12.11}$$

and
$$\overline{L_2} = \frac{l_2}{b_2} Y_2 = \frac{1}{wp} \left(\overline{\overline{\alpha}}_{t^p} + b_1 \overline{\overline{\beta}}_{t^p} \overline{u} - d_2 z \right) K_1, \tag{12.12}$$

while
$$L_1 = l_1 u K_1 \tag{12.13}$$

and
$$L_2 = \frac{1}{wp} \left[(\alpha_{t^p} + b_1 \beta_{t^p} u) h(u) - d_2 z \right] K_1. \tag{12.14}$$

Here α_{t^p} and β_{t^p} are given by (9.9) and (9.10) with $t^p = 0$, while
$$\overline{\overline{\beta}}_{t^p} = \frac{1}{\overline{\overline{k}}} \left(1 - \frac{wl_1}{b_1} \right) p \left(1 - t^p \right) \tag{12.15}$$

and
$$\overline{\overline{\alpha}}_{t^p} = \delta - \frac{d_1 + \delta \left(1 - t^p \right)}{\overline{\overline{k}}}; \tag{12.16}$$

here
$$\overline{\overline{k}} = 1 + b_1 \overline{s} p \tag{12.17}$$

If we assume that the unemployment benefit is a fixed proportion of the wage that the unemployed worker earned before loosing his job, then
$$B_U = (1 - \sigma) \, wpU. \tag{12.18}$$

Using (12.10), (12.11), (12.12), (12.13), and (12.14) we may give (12.18) the form
$$B_U = (1 - \sigma) \left(\overline{W_1} + \overline{W_2} - W_1 - W_2 \right), \tag{12.19}$$

where
$$\overline{W_1} = l_1 wp \overline{u} K_1 \tag{12.20}$$

and

$$\overline{W_2} = \left(\overline{\overline{\alpha}}_{t^p} + b_1 \overline{\overline{\beta}}_{t^p} \overline{u} - d_2 z\right) K_1 \tag{12.21}$$

are the total wages the two sectors would pay if equilibrium prevailed, while W_1 and W_2 are the total wages currently paid in the two sectors.

Substituting (12.20), (12.21), (3.20), (3.20), and (9.19) with $t^p = 0$ into (12.19) we obtain the benefit expenses in terms of the capacity utilization rate and the inventory level

$$
\begin{aligned}
B_U \;=\; & (1-\sigma)\, wl_1 p \left(\overline{u} - u\right) K_1 + \\
& (1-\sigma) \left(\overline{\overline{\alpha}}_{t^p} + b_1 \overline{\overline{\beta}}_{t^p} \overline{u} - (\alpha_{t^p} + b_1 \beta_{t^p} u)\, h(u)\right) K_1.
\end{aligned}
\tag{12.22}
$$

12.2.3 Demand for consumption goods

Finally, inserting (3.12), (3.22), (3.4), (9.19), (12.8), and (12.22) into (9.6), we obtain the demand for consumption goods

$$
\begin{aligned}
D_1 \;=\; & d_1 K_1 + d_2 K_2 + wl_1 up K_1 + \\
& [(\alpha_{t^p} + b_1 \beta_{t^p} u)\, h(u) - d_2 z]\, K_1 + \\
& (1-\sigma)\, \frac{wl_1 p\left(\overline{u} - u\right) + \overline{\overline{\alpha}}_{t^p} + b_1 \overline{\overline{\beta}}_{t^p} \overline{u} - (\alpha_{t^p} + b_1 \beta_{t^p} u)\, h(u)}{p}\, K_1.
\end{aligned}
\tag{12.23}
$$

Thus the differential system describing the evolution of the four variables u, s, p, z is again of the form (11.14), where now the function G is given by

$$
\begin{aligned}
G(u, s, p) \;=\; & \frac{k}{b_1 p} \left(\alpha_{t^p} + b_1 \beta_{t^p} u\right) \left(1 - h(u)\right) - \\
& \frac{(1-\sigma)}{b_1 p} \left(wl_1 p\left(\overline{u} - u\right) + \overline{\overline{\alpha}}_{t^p} + b_1 \overline{\overline{\beta}}_{t^p} \overline{u} - (\alpha_{t^p} + b_1 \beta_{t^p} u)\, h(u)\right),
\end{aligned}
\tag{12.24}
$$

while the function H is again given by (11.7).

12.2.4 Equilibria

Theorem 14 *All the normal equilibria $(\overline{u}, \overline{s}, \overline{p}, \overline{z})$ in the sense of (12.3) are equilibrium points of the differential system (11.14) when G and H are respectively given by (12.24) and (11.7) and conversely. If*

$$
h'(\overline{u}) < \frac{\dfrac{\partial F}{\partial u} \dfrac{(b_1 - wl_1)\, \overline{up}}{\overline{k}^2} + (1 - wl_1 \overline{s} p)}{\dfrac{\partial F}{\partial s} \, \overline{s} \left(\alpha_{t^p} + b_1 \overline{\beta}_{t^p} \overline{u}\right)}.
\tag{12.25}
$$

These equilibrium points are locally stable provided that

$$0 < \sigma < \overline{\sigma}, \tag{12.26}$$

where

$$\overline{\sigma} = \frac{\dfrac{\overline{\partial F}}{\partial u}\dfrac{(b_1 - wl_1)\,\overline{up} - d_1 - \delta}{\overline{k}^2} + (1 - wl_1\overline{s}p)}{\left(\dfrac{\overline{\alpha}_{t^p} + b_1\overline{\beta}_{t^p}\overline{u}}{b_1p}h'(u) + \dfrac{wl_1\overline{s}p}{\overline{k}}\overline{u}\right)\dfrac{\overline{\partial F}}{\partial s}}. \tag{12.27}$$

The proof is in the appendix 19.14.

As in all the preceding cases, theorem 14 can be extended to the case of a small positive profit tax rate t^p.

12.2.5 Is the budget deficit sustainable?

It is not to be forgotten that the significance of all the preceding discussion on different expansionary strategies depends on the assumption of perfect elasticity of the demand for government bonds[2].

Since our model does dot explicitly include the monetary side of the economy, we can not give a quantitative estimate of the outstanding debt and its impact on the interest rate; nevertheless we can sketch some qualitative considerations.

We have already observed[3] that a sizable accumulation of loanable funds takes place during the depression, thus it is perfectly conceivable that at least a part of these funds might be temporarily invested in government bonds issued to finance the expansive policy. As soon as an upswing begins[4] and the economy enters in an expansion phase the increase of tax rates[5] rises the tax revenue and allows the government to reduce or even to cancel the debt stock.

---

[2] See subsection 10.3.3

[3] See subsections 6.1.1, 2.2.3, and especially subsection 7.2.2.

[4] This may happen for instance as a consequence of a technical innovation as shown in subsections 7.2.2 and 7.3.2, as well as a result of an increase of foreign demand as explained in section 14.2 and subsection 13.3.2 .

[5] See chapter 11.

Part IV

The Open Economy: Importing from a Developing Country

Till now we have treated the case of a closed economy; in this part we want to extend our model to some cases of open economy.

An exhaustive discussion of the problems arising in an open economy would require a multi-country model, capable of taking into account phenomena such as product specialization of each country, exchange rates among different currencies, capital movements, etc. It is clear that it is impossible to deal with all the above mentioned facts in the framework of a model treating both capital goods and consumption goods as overall aggregates; thus our simple model would require substantial changes and generalizations which are outside the scope of this work.

Our aim here is to provide an overview of some problems arising when a large developed country imports some consumption goods from a small backward one and the latter imports capital goods from the former.

In chapter 13 we describe the stylized economy that we want to examine. In chapter 14 we introduce the generalizations of our model and discuss the new assumptions. Chapters 15 and 16 are devoted to the discussion of the changes in the equilibrium positions in the large country, caused by the ongoing development process in the small country. We discuss how the stabilizing policies, proved effective in the closed economy case, have to be adapted in order to work correctly also in the new context. We end this part collecting some remarks in chapter 17

13 Industrialization in an Open Economy

13.1   Large country and small country

The model developed so far describes a closed economy of a fully self-sufficient country where it is possible to project and produce all instrumental goods necessary to guarantee the flow of final goods demanded for domestic consumption. It is natural to assume that we are dealing with a large advanced country where all knowledge and skills, necessary to operate an advanced technology, are present.

In this section we want to enlarge our picture and consider also a small country, where an industrialization has started. On account of the lack of knowledge and skills characterizing this more backwards context, it is impossible to produce technologically advanced instrumental goods, therefore they are imported from the advanced country and then exploited to produce competitive consumer goods. A steady flow of imports of capital goods is feasible only if a parallel flow of exports of consumption goods can be generated toward the advanced country; thus the production of competitive consumption goods in the small country is exclusively, or at least mainly, destined to exports.

On account of the smallness of the developing country it is natural to assume that agents in the large country do not change their choice criteria[1]. Thus we maintain the assumptions[2] on the main features of the economy

---

[1]Described in chapter 2.

[2]See chapter 3 .

of the large country and devote this chapter do describe the economy of the small country and its interactions with that of the large one.

13.2 Dual structure of the small country

Describing the industrialization process of less developed economies it is usual "to imagine these economies as consisting of two distinct sectors, modern and traditional, and thus having a dual structure"[3].

13.2.1 Traditional and modern sectors

The traditional sector consists of a labor surplus, backward agricultural sector possibly sided by an old obsolete industrial sector, largely based on homemade technology and generally employing low quality labor and intermediate inputs. The modern sector is a generally small, new industrial sector employing up-to-date technology invented and produced in the developed country, sufficient to keep it relatively close to the developed country's technology frontier.

As usual in many surplus labor models, the expansion of the modern sector is feasible by transferring part of the labor force from the traditional one. Thus the labor is assumed to be in perfect elastic supply for the modern sector and the wage rate is near to subsistence level. The new sector has been created importing an initial stock of capital goods from the developed country in order to produce a flow of export of consumption goods.

13.2.2 The technology in the developed country and in the backward one

Also during the development process new plants are imported from the large country and produced to order by the same capital goods sector producing instrumental goods for the industrial sector of the large country itself. The technique embodied in these capital goods is obviously the most profitable one in the developed environment, but need not to be appropriate at the more backward context. Anyway importing up-to-date capital goods increases technical efficiency and set up a process a learning by doing in the small country.

Thus the modern sector in the small country operate the same technology as the consumption goods sector in the large country even if it can not be run as efficiently because of lack of specific skills, complementarities, and externalities that characterize a developed context. Thus even

---

[3]See Gomulka (1986) p. 171. A similar approach has been adopted by Cantalupi Nardini and Ricottilli (1992).

using identical technology, the plants in the developed country employ less workers and produce more output than do those in the backward one.

13.3   The modern sector in the small country

13.3.1   Price and production decisions in the small country

On account of its smallness we assume that the backward country is price taker both on the consumption goods market and on the capital goods one. In our model this means that prices in both sectors are decided by firms of the developed country (see subsections 2.2.1, 2.3.2, 3.2.1, 3.3.3); on the other hand firms in the small country do not need to hold stocks in order to offset price changes and thus their inventories are always near their equilibrium value. Therefore we can skip the inventory level in the small country from the key variables of our model and regard it as constant.

Given the reality of many developing countries, a market outlet for products of the new industrial sector is not something to be given for granted. The goods produced in the small country are only imperfect substitutes for those produced in the large one. Hence the major part of the demand for consumption goods in the large country is for domestically produced goods, while at most a small percentage may be fulfilled by imported goods, provided that their prices are sufficiently lower that those prevailing for domestically produced goods.

On the other hand, no demand for the bundle of modern consumption goods arises from workers in the small country; on account of the low per capita earnings they spend all their income on goods produced by the preexisting apparatus. This is certainly true at the beginning of the industrialization process, but may progressively change in successive phases. We are going to discuss briefly also this case (see chapter 17).

13.3.2   Investment decisions in the small country

At the initial stage all the domestic production of the small country is hardly sufficient for subsistence; thus it can not generate exports in exchange of the initial stock of capital of the modern sector. This may be purchased by obtaining a loan in the developed country, but even this may be hardly feasible in many realities because of the inherent risks and the consequent high interest rates. In many cases the beginning of the industrialization process is made possible by a deliberate political act of the government that offers incentives to investors such as contributions to the debt service, at least at the beginning of the process[4].

---

[4]Such an assumption rises the problem of threat posed by the debt burden to the growth of the small country. We do not deal directly with this problem here, but we

In the subsequent periods we assume that also in the small country a part of the profit of the modern sector is spent on the market of modern consumption goods and the other part, if any, is reinvested in the sector itself. After all the entrepreneurs of the new modern sector of the small country are an emerging class, aiming at achieving a standard of life similar to that prevailing in the developed country. Alternatively it is also conceivable that they are citizen of the large country, searching for new opportunities in the small one.

refer to Cantalupi Nardini Ricottilli (1992) for a discussion of its financial and structural aspects. In Chapter we give some hints in this direction.

14 The Developed Country and the Developing one

This chapter parallels in some sense chapter 4, where the formalism of the portrayed economy has been developed under the assumption that the economy is closed. Here we introduce all the necessary changes for the case of an open economy, as described in the preceding chapter 13.

14.1 The new industrial sector in the small country

14.1.1 Input, output, and profit

Coherently with section 3.2.1, we denote by Y_e, L_e, and K_e output and inputs (of labor and capital, respectively) of the new industrial sector in the small country. Analogously we denote aggregate wage bill, profit, and ex ante investment of that sector by W_e, Π_e, and I_e^a.

Since we are assuming that the modern sector of the small country operates the same technology as the consumption goods sector in the large country, but in a developing context it can not be run so efficiently as there, we again represent the productive process by a Leontiev production function (see section 3.1)

$$Y_e = \min\left\{ b_e K_e, \frac{b_e}{l_e} L_e \right\}, \tag{14.1}$$

where the productivity of capital b_e and the productivity of labor $\frac{b_e}{l_e}$ are below the respective values b_1 and $\frac{b_1}{l_1}$ obtained in the advanced context.

Also the real wage rate w_e, paid to workers in the modern sector of the developing country, is below (possibly much below) the value w prevailing in the large country.

In order that the production is feasible it is necessary that the surplus condition (analogous to (3.5))

$$Y_e p_e - W_e > 0 \qquad (14.2)$$

holds. Also in this case this condition may be considered a compatibility condition (see (3.6)) of the real wage rate with the productive technology

$$\frac{b_e}{l_e} > w_e. \qquad (14.3)$$

Thus the aggregate wage bill paid by the modern sector in the developing country is (see (3.4))

$$W_e = w_e L_e p_e, \qquad (14.4)$$

where p_e denotes the price of (the bundle of) consumption goods produced there.

Assuming that the depreciation rate of fixed capital in the small country is the same as in the large one[1], the size of the new industrial sector evolves according to (see (3.3))

$$\dot{K}_e = I_e - \delta K_e. \qquad (14.5)$$

Also in the present case we assume that the capital goods installed in the small country are specific and can not be transferred to either sector in the large one and conversely. Thus only new capital goods are traded and exported.

The profit generated by the modern sector is (see (3.10))

$$\Pi_e = Y_e p_e - (W_e + \delta K_e p_2). \qquad (14.6)$$

Also in this case (see (3.11)) we assume that the profit is divided into two parts: consumed and accumulated parts

$$\Pi_e = \Pi_e^c + \Pi_e^a, \qquad (14.7)$$

where the consumed part Π_e^c is proportional (see (3.12)) to the fixed capital K_e installed in the modern sector

$$\Pi_e^c = d_e K_e p_2 \qquad (14.8)$$

Obviously the remuneration rate d_e of capital invested in the developing country is different from that prevailing in the same sector of the developing one d_1. On account of the higher riskiness that such investment generally entails d_e is generally larger (possibly much larger) that d_2.

---

[1]This assumption is by no means restrictive and can be easily removed with minor changes.

14.1.2 Investment

We are assuming that the accumulated profit (if any) of the new industrial sector Π_e^a is reinvested in the sector itself, unless the sector does not generate enough profit to pay the scheduled dividends (14.8); thus the ex-ante investment (see (3.32)) is given by

$$I_e^a = \max\left\{\delta K_e + \frac{\Pi_e^a}{p_2}, 0\right\} \tag{14.9}$$

Obviously the capital goods sector of the developed country produces to order also for the modern sector of the small country, thus its output Y_2 coincides with the demand D_2, unless the productive capacity of the sector is insufficient (see (3.24)). Since the demand D_2 is the sum of the demand coming from the developed country plus that coming from the developing one, we have

$$D_2 = I_1^a + I_2 + I_e^a. \tag{14.10}$$

If $D_2 \leq b_2 K_2$ all planned investment in the modern sector (14.9) can be effected and the ex ante investment I_e^a coincides with the ex-post investment I_e. If this is not the case, we assume that the demand coming from the developed country is satisfied first, while that coming from the small country is destined to remain partially unsatisfied. In this case the ex-post investment in the small country is given by

$$I_e = b_2 K_2 - (I_1^a + I_2), \tag{14.11}$$

if the right hand side of (14.11) is positive (in this case $I_1 = I_1^a$). Otherwise $I_e = 0$ and

$$I_1 = b_2 K_2 - I_2. \tag{14.12}$$

In both cases (14.11) and (14.12) firms in the capital goods sector of the advanced country react to disequilibrium in the capital goods market as described in subsection 3.3.3.

14.1.3 Prices and demand

We are assuming that the consumption goods produced in the small country are only imperfect substitutes of those produced in the large one and their competitiveness on the market in the large country obviously depend on the gap between their price p_e and the price p_1 of domestically produced goods. We assume that firms of the modern sector in the small country maintain a constant gap that guarantees a constant share of the market. Thus

$$p_e = (1 - \zeta)p_1 \tag{14.13}$$

and

$$D_e = \varepsilon D_T, \tag{14.14}$$

where D_T is the total demand for consumption goods, while D_e is the demand for goods produced in the small country. Obviously ε depends on ζ.

The total demand D_T is the sum of the demand of workers employed in both sectors of the large country plus the demand of capitalists of either country plus the purchases of the government of the large country

$$D_T = \frac{\Pi_1^c + \Pi_2^c + \Pi_e^c + W_1 + W_2 - T^c + B + P}{p_1} \tag{14.15}$$

Since we are assuming that workers in the small country spend all their income on goods produced by the traditional sector, it is natural to assume that the fiscal policy of the government of the small country has no effects on the demand D_T of modern consumption goods. In what follows by "the government" we steadily indicate the government of the developed country.

Assumption (14.13), (14.14) is very strong indeed; it is hardly acceptable in the long run, but may be a good approximation in the short-medium run, provided that the economy of the large country is experiencing a regular expansion and thus the total demand D_T does not oscillate too much.

Since firms in the small country do not hold stocks to offset possible excess demand, the demand D_e may remain partially unsatisfied if the productive capacity of the modern sector is not enough; thus[2]

$$Y_e = \begin{array}{ll} b_e K_e & \text{if } D_e > b_e K_e \\ D_e & \text{if } D_e \leq b_e K_e \end{array} \tag{14.16}$$

Obviuosly the demand for goods produced in the large country is

$$D_1 = D_T - Y_e \tag{14.17}$$

14.2   Early phase and further phase

It would be of great interest to know how the two regimes (14.16) alternate, but in general it is impossible to fix a typical sequence of them, since it depend on the evolution of the economy of the large country. However, if the economy of the large country is expands regularly for a fairly long time, it is reasonable to assume that at the beginning of the industrialization process the capital stock in the modern sector of the developing country is still under-dimensioned and $D_e > b_e K_e$, whereas after a suitable expansion period a constant flow of investment has increased it and the second regime prevails.

---

[2]The full performance of the modern sector of the small country is assumed throughout in Cantalupi Nardini and Ricottilli (1992).

Since we are going to analyze mainly this case, we call the first regime (14.16) early phase of the industrialization process, while we call further phase the second one.

Here we have not described the preparatory phase: i.e. the period when the initial capital stock of the modern sector of the small country is produced and installed. Obviously the increase in the demand for exported capital goods may exert sizeable growth effects in the developed country. Since this type of demand is often based on export credits granted by the exporting country, a suitable timing in offering these credits may allow the developed country to overcome a recession phase.

15 Perturbation of Equilibria and Stabilization Policies: the Early Phase

In this chapter and in chapter 16 we introduce the new dynamical system, describing the evolution of the economies of either country during the early and further phase of the industrialization process of the small country. This allows us to analyze how the equilibrium points, we have found in the closed economy case (see chapter (5)), are perturbed by the import export flows and how the government has to modify its stabilization policies in order to preserve their effectiveness.

15.1 Large and small country during the early phase

15.1.1 The modern sector in the developing country

During the early phase the demand for imported consumption goods in the large country exceeds the productive capacity of the modern sector of the small country, thus (see (14.1) and (14.4)) production, employment, and total wages in this sector are give by

$$Y_e = b_e K_e, \tag{15.1}$$

$$L_e = l_e K_e, \tag{15.2}$$

$$W_e = w_e l_e K_e p_e. \tag{15.3}$$

The net profit of the modern sector can easily be obtained substituting (15.1) and (15.3) into (14.6)

$$\Pi_e = ((b_e - w_e l_e) p_e - \delta p_2) K_e, \tag{15.4}$$

where we have maintained the assumption that the depreciation rate in the developing country is the same as in the developed one.

From (15.4) and (14.8) we obtain the accumulated profit

$$\Pi_e^a = ((b_e - w_e l_e) p_e - (\delta + d_e) p_2) K_e, \tag{15.5}$$

and the ex-ante investment (see (14.9)) in the modern sector of the small country

$$I_e^a = \left((b_e - w_e l_e) \frac{p_e}{p_2} - (\delta + d_e) \right) K_e. \tag{15.6}$$

15.1.2   The large country

We pass now to the effects of the industrialization process on either sectors of the developed country. Extending the approach of section 4.1, we express all relevant economic quantities by means of the stock of fixed capital in the consumption goods sector of the large country and five relative variables: the productive capacity utilization rate u (see (3.15)), the inventory level s (see (3.7)), the relative price p (see (4.1)), the relative capitalization z (see (4.2)), and the relative capitalization of the modern sector in the developing country with respect to the capitalization of the consumption goods sector in the developed one

$$z_e = \frac{K_e}{K_1} \tag{15.7}$$

We notice explicitly that, thanks to assumption (15.8) below, the relative price of imported consumption goods with respect to the price of (domestically produced) capital goods is simply

$$\frac{p_e}{p_2} = p(1 - \zeta) \tag{15.8}$$

The capital goods sector

Taking into account (14.10) and (15.6), the production of capital goods Y_2 in the developed country can be obtained along the same lines which led to formula (4.16)

$$Y_2 = \frac{b_2}{w l_2 p} \left[(\alpha + b_1 \beta u) h(u) + (1 - \zeta)(b_e - w_e l_e) p z_e - d_2 z - d_e z_e \right] K_1 \tag{15.9}$$

Obviousliy (15.9) holds under the assumption that

$$D_2 \leq b_2 K_2, \tag{15.10}$$

i.e. capital goods are not rationed and all sectors are profitable both in the large country and in the small one. As far as the large country is concerned, this means that condition (4.21) holds; on the other hand, the profitability condition for the modern sector in the small country reads

$$(b_e - w_e l_e)(1 - \zeta) p - d_e > 0 \tag{15.11}$$

Condition (15.11) is satisfied unless the relative price p falls below the critical value $\frac{d_e}{(b_e - w_e l_e)(1 - \zeta)}$; this may happen if the economy of the developed country falls into a depression phase. It is fairly natural to assume that the beginning of the industrialization is undertaken during an expansion phase or, at least, during a stability phase in that country. Moreover, since our interest is the present analysis is mainly for the case when the evolution of the large economy is sufficiently regular, we are going the consider only situations where the relative price p is almost constant and (15.11) holds.

Analogously the total wages paid by the capital goods sector (see (4.17)) is now

$$W_2 = [(\alpha + b_1 \beta u) h(u) + \tag{15.12}$$
$$(1 - \zeta)(b_e - w_e l_e) p z_e - d_2 z - d_e z_e] K_1.$$

Finally we calculate the investment in the capital goods sector of the large country simply substituting (15.9) into (4.13)

$$I_2 = \left(\frac{b_2}{w l_2 p} - 1\right) [(\alpha + b_1 \beta u) h(u) - (1 - \zeta)(b_e - w_e l_e) p z_e - d_e z_e] K_1 -$$
$$\frac{b_2}{w l_2 p} d_2 K_2. \tag{15.13}$$

It is clear that also (15.12) and (15.13) hold if profitability and non rationing conditions (3.27), (15.11), and (15.10) hold.

The consumption goods sector

Under the assumption of the preceding subsection 15.1.2, the demand for consumption goods (see 14.15) is given by

$$D_T = \frac{1}{p} \Big[w l_1 p u + (\alpha + b_1 \beta u) h(u) + d_1 - \tag{15.14}$$
$$(b_e - w_e l_e)(1 - \zeta) p z_e + \frac{B + P - T^c}{K_1} \Big] K_1.$$

Inserting (15.11) and (15.1) into (14.17) we obtain the demand for consumption goods produced in the developed country

$$D_1 = \frac{1}{p} \Big[w l_1 p u + (\alpha + b_1 \beta u) h(u) + d_1 - \tag{15.15}$$
$$(\zeta b_e + (1 - \zeta) w_e l_e) p z_e + \frac{B + P - T^c}{K_1} \Big] K_1.$$

Formulas (4.24) and (15.15) yield the evolution of the inventory level s (see (4.25))

$$
\frac{ds}{dt} = \frac{k}{b_1 p} \left(\alpha + b_1 \beta u \right) \left(1 - h(u) \right) + \tag{15.16}
$$

$$
\frac{1}{b_1 p} \left[\left(\zeta b_e + (1 - \zeta) w_e l_e \right) p z_e - \frac{B + P - T^c}{K_1} \right].
$$

15.2   The dynamical system

Now we are in position to specify the dynamical system during the early phase. Since we are assuming that firms in the small country are price takers (see subsection 13.3.1), the decisions on prices and production of firms in either sector of the large country are not directly affected by the flux of imports, thus prices and outputs of these firms are still described by subsections 3.2.1, 3.2.2, and 3.3.2, 3.3.3 for consumption and capital goods sector respectively.

15.2.1   Relative sizes of the sectors

To complete the description of the evolution of the economy we need only to determine how the sectors grow with respect to one another.

Growth of the capital goods sector with respect to the consumption goods sector in the large country

Substituting (4.9) and (15.13) into (3.3) the evolution of the relative capitalization z is easily obtained

$$
\frac{dz}{dt} = \frac{b_2 - w l_2 p}{w l_2 p} \left[(\alpha + b_1 \beta u) h(u) + (b_e - w_e l_e)(1 - \zeta) p z_e - d_e z_e \right] -
$$

$$
\left[\frac{b_2}{w l_2 p} + (\alpha + b_1 \beta u) h(u) \right] z. \tag{15.17}
$$

Growth of the modern sector in the small country with respect to the consumption goods sector in the large country

Analogously, substituting (4.9) and (15.6) into (14.5), we obtain the evolution of the relative capitalization z_e (see (15.7))

$$
\frac{dz_e}{dt} = \left[(b_e - w_e l_e)(1 - \zeta) p - d_e - (\alpha + b_1 \beta u) h(u) \right] z_e. \tag{15.18}
$$

15.2.2   The differential system

We conclude subsection 15.2 writing the differential system that describes the evolution of both economies during the early phase of the industrialization process of the small country

$$
\begin{cases}
\dot{u} &= F\left(u, s\right) \\[4pt]
\dot{s} &= \dfrac{k}{b_1 p}\left(\alpha + b_1 \beta u\right)\left(1 - h(u)\right) + \\
 &\quad \dfrac{1}{b_1 p}\left[\left(\zeta b_e + (1 - \zeta)\, w_e l_e\right) p z_e - \dfrac{B + P - T^c}{K_1}\right] \\[4pt]
\dot{p} &= g_1\left(s\right) p \\[4pt]
\dot{z} &= \dfrac{b_2 - w l_2 p}{w l_2 p}\left[\left(\alpha + b_1 \beta u\right) h(u) + \left(b_e - w_e l_e\right)\left(1 - \zeta\right) p z_e - d_e z_e\right] \\
 &\quad - \left[\dfrac{b_2}{w l_2 p} + \left(\alpha + b_1 \beta u\right) h(u)\right] z \\[4pt]
\dot{z}_e &\quad \left[\left(b_e - w_e l_e\right)\left(1 - \zeta\right) p - d_e - \left(\alpha + b_1 \beta u\right) h(u)\right] z_e
\end{cases}
$$

$$\text{(15.19)}$$

15.3   Equilibrium and fiscal policies

15.3.1   Balancing the budget

An easy inspection of the differential system (15.19) shows that if the government simply balances its budget by means of the consumption tax

$$T^c = B + P \tag{15.20}$$

no equilibrium can ever be reached; in fact, if $u = \bar{u}$ and $s = \bar{s}$, then $\dot{u} = 0$ and $\dot{p} = 0$, but $\dot{s} > 0$; conversely, if $\dot{s} = 0$ and $\dot{p} = 0$, then $\dot{u} < 0$, while if $\dot{u} = 0$ and $\dot{s} = 0$, then $\dot{p} > 0$.

15.3.2   Deficit spending and existence of an equilibrium

It is clear that an equilibrium can be achieved only if the government implements a fiscal policy designed to offset both the intrinsic instability of the economy of the developed country (see chapter 5) and the perturbations caused by the import-export flows. This can be done, for instance, introducing a program of unemployment benefits to be financed by deficit spending[1], as described in section 12.2, and increasing direct purchases on the market of consumption goods beyond the revenue of the consumption tax. In detail

$$B = \bar{B} + B_U \tag{15.21}$$

---

[1] We maintain the assumption of perfect elasticity of the demand for government bonds, introduced in subsection 10.3.3.

and

$$P = T^c - \bar{B} + (\zeta b_e + (1 - \zeta) w_e l_e) p z_e K_1. \tag{15.22}$$

In (15.21) and (15.22) $\bar{B}$ denotes the permanent part of transfer payments to households, to be financed by tax revenue, while B_U is the total amount of the temporary unemployment benefits, to be paid during depressions, as explained in subsection 12.2.2 (see equation (12.19)).

If the government takes both actions (15.21) and (15.22) utilization rate u and inventory level s stabilize to their normal levels and thus so does the relative price p.

Remark 25 *It may be interesting to briefly discuss the effects of each action separately.*

If the government introduces the unemployment benefits (15.21), but does not increases the direct purchases $\left(P = T^c - \bar{B} \right)$, then the utilization rate converges to a value below the normal one, while the inventory level settles to a value above the normal one. Thus the overall effect is to stabilize the economy in a depression that in the medium run will undermine the profitability of firms in both countries.

On the other hand, if the government increases the direct transfers as indicated in (15.22) without introducing unemployment benefits, the point $(\bar{u}, \bar{s}, \bar{p})$ is an equilibrium for the three variables (u, s, p), but it is unstable.

Till now we have described the evolution of the variables u, s, and p when the fiscal policy is (15.21) and (15.22). Now we pass to include also z and z_e in our analysis.

Theorem 15 *The differential system (15.19) has at least an equilibrium point $(\bar{u}, \bar{s}, \bar{p}, \bar{z}, \bar{z}_e)$.*

Proof From (15.18) it is clear that there exists at least a value $\bar{p}$ of the relative price satisfying the following equation in the unknown variable p

$$(b_e - w_e l_e)(1 - \zeta) p - d_e - \left(\bar{\bar{\alpha}} + b_1 \bar{\bar{\beta}} \bar{u} \right) = 0; \tag{15.23}$$

(we remember that $\bar{\bar{\alpha}}$ and $\bar{\bar{\beta}}$ are functions of p, see equations (12.15) (12.16)).

On the other hand, by equation (15.17), the equilibrium value $\bar{z}$ for the fourth variable z is given by

$$\bar{z} = \frac{b_2 - w l_2 \, \bar{p} \left(\bar{\alpha} + b_1 \, \bar{\beta} \bar{u} \right) + (b_e - w_e l_e)(1 - \zeta) \, \bar{p} \bar{z}_e - d_e \, \bar{z}_e}{w l_2 \, \bar{p}} \cdot \frac{1}{\dfrac{b_2}{w l_2 \, \bar{p}} + \left(\bar{\alpha} + b_1 \, \bar{\beta} \bar{u} \right)}.$$
$$\tag{15.24}$$

It is clear that all points $(\bar{u}, \bar{s}, \bar{p}, \bar{z}, \bar{z}_e)$ satisfying (15.23) and (15.24) are equilibrium points of the system (15.19) where P, B, and T^c are given by (15.21) and (15.22).

16 Perturbation of Equilibria and Stabilization Policies: the Further Phase

16.1 Catching up and falling behind

The economic relevance of the equilibrium points found in theorem 15 is not to be overestimated. Even if the economy of the developed country is in equilibrium before the beginning of the industrialization process in the backward one thanks to the implementation of some stabilization policies as those discussed in chapters 11 and 12, it is clear that this equilibrium will survive if and only if the technical ad economic parameters b_e, w_e, l_e, d_e, ζ, and the relative size z_e of the modern sector in the small country satisfy conditions (15.23) and (15.24) at the very beginning of the early phase, where $\bar{u}$, $\bar{s}$, $\bar{p}$, $\bar{z}$ are the values characterizing the preexisting equilibrium (5.1).

This is very unlikely to happen, since it would require that all economic choices and technical conditions of the modern sector in the developing country were perfectly adapted to the equilibrium prevailing in the large country.

There are two possible alternative to the continuation of the preexisting equilibrium into (15.23) (15.24): either

$$(b_e - w_e l_e)\,(1 - \zeta)\,p - d_e - (\alpha + b_1 \beta u)\,h(u) > 0 \qquad (16.1)$$

or

$$(b_e - w_e l_e)\,(1 - \zeta)\,p - d_e - (\alpha + b_1 \beta u)\,h(u) < 0 \qquad (16.2)$$

If (16.2) holds at the beginning of the early phase, then prices, inventories, and utilization capacity in the large country remain unchanged at their equilibrium values, but the rate of growth of the modern sector in the small country is less that the rate of growth of the overall economy of the large country. Thus the relative size of the small country z_e with respect to the large one decreases an eventually converges to zero and the economy of the large country resembles more and more a closed one.

On the other hand, if (16.1) holds at the beginning of the early phase, then again prices, inventories, and utilization capacity in the large country remain unchanged at their equilibrium values, but now the modern sector of the small country grows quicker that both sectors in the large one. Thus the early phase is a catching up phase for the small country: the productive capacity of the modern sector expands rapidly and soon the further phase begins, at least as long as the government of the developed country can and will maintain the stabilization policy (15.22) despite it causes increasing budget deficits[1].

Chapter 16 is devoted to the analysis of the further phase. We again restrict this analysis to the case when all sectors are profitable in both countries and there is no rationing; i.e. (4.21) (15.11) hold and $D_2 \leq b_2 K_2$.

16.2   Large and small country during the further phase

In contrast with section 15.1, we begin our discussion of the further phase analyzing the economy of the large country.

16.2.1   The large country

Capital goods sector

Taking into account (15.16), (9.11), (9.16), (15.6) again, we obtain the output of the capital goods sector

$$Y_2 = \left(1 - \frac{wl_2p}{b_2}\right) Y_2 - d_2 K_2 + (\alpha + b_1 \beta u) h(u) K_1 + \quad (16.3)$$
$$(1 - \zeta)\left(1 - \frac{w_e l_e}{b_e}\right) pY_e - d_e K_e,$$

On the other hand

$$Y_e = D_e = \varepsilon D_T. \quad (16.4)$$

since now we are assuming that the second of (14.16) holds.

Thus we are able to write output Y_2 and total wages W_2 of the capital goods sector as functions of the relative variables introduced in subsection

---

[1] We postpone the discussion of this problem to chapter 17 at the end of this part.

15.1.2, the stock of fixed capital of the consumption goods sector in the large country, and the demand D_T for consumption goods

$$Y_2 = \frac{b_2}{wl_2p}$$

(16.5)

$$\left[(\alpha + b_1\beta u)\,h\,(u) - d_2z - d_ez_e + \varepsilon\,(1 - \zeta)\left(1 - \frac{w_el_e}{b_e}\right)p\frac{D_T}{K_1}\right]K_1$$

$$W_2 =$$

(16.6)

$$\left[(\alpha + b_1\beta u)\,h\,(u) - d_2z - d_ez_e + \varepsilon\,(1 - \zeta)\left(1 - \frac{w_el_e}{b_e}\right)p\frac{D_T}{K_1}\right]K_1$$

The consumption goods sector

Formula (16.6) yields the last component of the demand for consumption goods (14.15), after (3.4), (3.12), (3.22), and (14.8); substituting into (14.15) we get

$$D_T = \frac{1}{1 - \varepsilon\,(1 - \zeta)\left(1 - \frac{w_el_e}{b_e}\right)}\frac{1}{p}$$

(16.7)

$$\left[wl_1pu + (\alpha + b_1\beta u)\,h\,(u) + d_1 + \frac{B + P - T^c}{K_1}\right]K_1$$

Exploiting again (16.4) and (14.17) it is easy to write the evolution of the inventory level

$$\frac{ds}{dt} = \frac{k}{b_1p}\,(\alpha + b_1\beta u)\,(1 - h(u)) +$$

(16.8)

$$\varepsilon\,(1 - \zeta)\frac{1}{b_1p}\frac{\frac{w_el_e}{b_e}}{1 - \varepsilon\,(1 - \zeta)\left(1 - \frac{w_el_e}{b_e}\right)}\,[wl_1pu + (\alpha + b_1\beta u)\,h\,(u) + d_1] -$$

$$\frac{1 - \varepsilon\,(1 - \zeta)}{1 - \varepsilon\,(1 - \zeta)\left(1 - \frac{w_el_e}{b_e}\right)}\frac{B + P - T^c}{b_1pK_1}$$

16.3   The dynamical system

As in section 15.2, the dynamical system during the further phase is completely specified as soon as we know the evolution of the relative sizes of sectors in both countries.

16.3.1 Relative sizes

Substituting (16.5) into (4.13) and using (16.7), we obtain the evolution of the investment in the capital goods sector in the large country as a function of the fiscal policy of the government of the large country

$$
I_2 = \left[\frac{b_2 - wl_2p}{wl_2p} \frac{(\alpha + b_1\beta u)\, h\,(u)}{1 - \varepsilon\,(1-\zeta)\left(1 - \dfrac{w_e l_e}{b_e}\right)} - \right.
$$

$$
\frac{b_2 d_2}{wl_2p} z - \frac{b_2 - wl_2p}{wl_2p} d_e z_e +
$$

$$
\left. \frac{b_2 - wl_2p}{wl_2p} \frac{\varepsilon\,(1-\zeta)\left(1 - \dfrac{w_e l_e}{b_e}\right)}{1 - \varepsilon\,(1-\zeta)\left(1 - \dfrac{w_e l_e}{b_e}\right)} \left(wl_1 pu + d_1 + \frac{B + P - T^c}{b_1 p K_1} \right) \right] K_1 \tag{16.9}
$$

From (16.9) and (3.3) it is easy to obtain

$$
\frac{dz}{dt} = \frac{b_2 - wl_2p}{wl_2p} \frac{(\alpha + b_1\beta u)\, h\,(u)}{1 - \varepsilon\,(1-\zeta)\left(1 - \dfrac{w_e l_e}{b_e}\right)} - \tag{16.10}
$$

$$
\left[\frac{b_2 d_2}{wl_2p} + (\alpha + b_1\beta u)\, h(u) \right] z - \frac{b_2 - wl_2p}{wl_2p} d_e z_e +
$$

$$
\frac{b_2 - wl_2p}{wl_2p} \frac{\varepsilon\,(1-\zeta)\left(1 - \dfrac{w_e l_e}{b_e}\right)}{1 - \varepsilon\,(1-\zeta)\left(1 - \dfrac{w_e l_e}{b_e}\right)} \left(wl_1 pu + d_1 + \frac{B + P - T^c}{b_1 p K_1} \right)
$$

Instead of (15.6) now we have

$$
I_e^a = \left[\left(1 - \frac{w_e l_e}{b_e}\right)(1-\zeta)\, p \frac{D_e}{K_1} - d_e z_e \right] K_1 \tag{16.11}
$$

Substituting (16.11) into (3.3) and having in mind that we are assuming that $I_e = I_e^a$, we obtain the evolution of the size of the modern sector in the small country

$$
\frac{dK_e}{dt} = \left[-\delta\zeta_e + \frac{\varepsilon\,(1-\zeta)\left(1 - \dfrac{w_e l_e}{b_e}\right)}{1 - \varepsilon\,(1-\zeta)\left(1 - \dfrac{w_e l_e}{b_e}\right)} \left(wl_1 pu + d_1 + \frac{B + P - T^c}{b_1 p K_1} \right) - d_e z_e \right] \tag{16.12}
$$

We eventually get the evolution of the new sector in the developing country with respect to the consumption goods sector in the developed one during the further phase

$$\frac{dz_e}{dt} = \frac{\varepsilon (1 - \zeta) \left(1 - \frac{w_e l_e}{b_e}\right)}{1 - \varepsilon (1 - \zeta) \left(1 - \frac{w_e l_e}{b_e}\right)}$$

$$\left(w l_1 p u + (\alpha + b_1 \beta u) h(u) + d_1 + \frac{B + P - T^c}{b_1 p K_1}\right) -$$

$$[d_e + (\alpha + b_1 \beta u) h(u)] z_e \qquad (16.13)$$

16.3.2   The differential system

As already observed above, the import-export flows do not directly affect production and price decisions of firms in the advanced country, thus we can write the differential system describing the evolution of both economies during the further phase of the industrialization process

$$\begin{cases}
\dot{u} = & F(u, s) \\
\dot{s} = & \frac{k}{b_1 p} (\alpha + b_1 \beta u) (1 - h(u)) + \\
& \varepsilon (1 - \zeta) \frac{1}{b_1 p} \dfrac{\frac{w_e l_e}{b_e}}{1 - \varepsilon (1 - \zeta)\left(1 - \frac{w_e l_e}{b_e}\right)} [w l_1 p u + (\alpha + b_1 \beta u) h(u) + d_1] - \\
& \dfrac{1 - \varepsilon (1 - \zeta)}{1 - \varepsilon (1 - \zeta)\left(1 - \frac{w_e l_e}{b_e}\right)} \frac{B + P - T^c}{b_1 p K_1} \\
\dot{p} = & g_1(s) p \\
\dot{z} = & \frac{b_2 - w l_2 p}{w l_2 p} \dfrac{(\alpha + b_1 \beta u) h(u)}{1 - \varepsilon (1 - \zeta)\left(1 - \frac{w_e l_e}{b_e}\right)} - \\
& \left[\frac{b_2 d_2}{w l_2 p} + (\alpha + b_1 \beta u) h(u)\right] z - \frac{b_2 - w l_2 p}{w l_2 p} d_e z_e + \\
& \frac{b_2 - w l_2 p}{w l_2 p} \dfrac{\varepsilon (1 - \zeta)\left(1 - \frac{w_e l_e}{b_e}\right)}{1 - \varepsilon (1 - \zeta)\left(1 - \frac{w_e l_e}{b_e}\right)} \left(w l_1 p u + d_1 + \frac{B + P - T^c}{b_1 p K_1}\right) \\
\dot{z}_e = & \dfrac{\varepsilon (1 - \zeta)\left(1 - \frac{w_e l_e}{b_e}\right)}{1 - \varepsilon (1 - \zeta)\left(1 - \frac{w_e l_e}{b_e}\right)} (w l_1 p u + (\alpha + b_1 \beta u) h(u) + \\
& d_1 + \frac{B + P - T^c}{b_1 p K_1}) - [d_e + (\alpha + b_1 \beta u) h(u)] z_e
\end{cases}$$

$$(16.14)$$

16.4   Equilibrium and fiscal policy

16.4.1   Balancing the budget

In full analogy with the results obtained in the case of the early phase (see subsection 15.3.1), also during the further phase no equilibrium exists if the government balances its budget (see (15.18)) by means of the consumption tax T^c.

16.4.2   Deficit spending and equilibrium

Again (see subsection 15.3.2), if the government aims at stabilizing the economy in the large country, it is necessary to design a fiscal policy with two different targets: contrasting the intrinsic instability of the economy of the large country and balancing the effects of the import-export flows.

The first target is achieved introducing a program of unemployment benefits as described in subsection 15.3.2 (see (15.21) and (12.19)), while the second target can be reached expanding the direct purchases of goods and services

$$P = T^c - \bar{B} + \frac{\varepsilon (1 - \zeta)}{1 - \varepsilon (1 - \zeta)} \frac{w_e l_e}{b_e} \left[w l_1 p u + (\alpha + b_1 \beta u) h (u) + d_1 \right] K_1$$
(16.15)

In this case

$$\frac{ds}{dt} = \frac{k}{b_1 p} (\alpha + b_1 \beta u) (1 - h(u)) -$$
(16.16)

$$\frac{1 - \varepsilon (1 - \zeta)}{1 - \varepsilon (1 - \zeta) \left(1 - \dfrac{w_e l_e}{b_e} \right)} \frac{1 - \sigma}{b_1 p}$$

$$\left[w l_1 p (\bar{u} - u) + \left(\bar{\bar{\alpha}} + b_1 \, \bar{\bar{\beta}} \bar{u} \right) - (\alpha + b_1 \beta u) h (u) \right].$$

Thus the government is able to stabilize prices, inventory level, and productive capacity utilization rate, whereas it is again[2] very unlikely that the relative proportions z and z_e are stationary, unless they already have very particular values at the beginning of the further phase (we again refer to the comments to theorem 15 that apply also to the present case).

16.5   Technical progress in the open economy

We conclude our overview on the stabilization policies in the open economy with a discussion on the effects of technical progress on the outcomes of

---

[2] See section 16.1.

these policies. Beside the four main types of technical progresses presented in the four sections of chapter 7^3, we have to consider technical progresses occurring in the new industrial sector in the developing country. Using the same notation as in section 7.2 we write

$$
Y_e = \begin{cases} \min\left\{ b_e^* K_e, \dfrac{b_e^*}{l_e^*} L_e \right\} & \text{for } t < 0 \\[2ex] \min\left\{ b_e K_e, \dfrac{b_e}{l_e} L_e \right\} & \text{for } t \geqslant 0 \end{cases} . \tag{16.17}
$$

If

$$
\begin{aligned}
l_e &< l_e^* \\
b_e &< b_e^*
\end{aligned} \tag{16.18}
$$

formula (16.17) represents an increase of the labor productivity in the developing country, whereas if

$$
\begin{aligned}
b_e &> b_e^* \\
\dfrac{b_e}{l_e} &= \dfrac{b_e^*}{l_e^*}
\end{aligned} \tag{16.19}
$$

it represents an increase of the capital productivity in the same new sector.

16.5.1   Early phase

If the productivity of labor jumps upward (see (16.17), (16.18)) in the new industrial sector of the developing country during the early phase the governmental direct purchases of goods and services (15.22), necessary to preserve the equilibrium, may be reduced

$$
P < P^* \tag{16.20}
$$

On the contrary, if the productivity of capital rises in the same sector (see (16.17), (16.19)), those purchases have to be increased

$$
P > P^* \tag{16.21}
$$

This result is not surprising since in the first case the technical progress results in an increase of profit for firms in the new sector, thanks to the wage rigidity[4]. Since the consumed part of this profit is spent on the consumption goods market in the developed country, the government may reduce its

---

[3]In the present context all these cases are to be understood as occurring in either sector of the developed country.

[4]Of course, if we assume that, at least after some time, workers in the new sector are able to obtain an increase of wages, this effect will be offset.

purchases of the same amount. A further beneficial though smaller effect on the activity levels of the industry in the large country is given by the increase of the demand for capital goods of firms of the new sector

In the second case the increase of profit of the new sector is not the only outcome of the change. In the early phase the output of the new sector is constrained by the productive capacity (see section 14.2) and the innovation weakens this constraint. Hence the sector may now produce and export more than before, increasing the perturbation of the economy of the large country.

16.5.2   The late phase

First of all we observe that either types of innovation discussed in the preceding subsection 16.5.1 play in favor of the catching up process (see section 16.1). A specular mechanism unfolds if the productivity of either labor or capital jumps up in the consumption goods sector in the large country; in this case a falling behind outcome becomes more probable[5]. All these results are quite natural since we are dealing with two sectors competing with one another.

Also in the further phase[6] an increase of the labor productivity allows the government of the large country to diminish the stabilizing intervention (16.15)

$$P < P^* \tag{16.22}$$

The analogy with the early phase breaks down in the case of an increase of capital productivity, as during the further phase the output Y_e is not constrained by the productive capacity any longer and thus the innovation has no immediate effect on the stabilizing policy. Of course the increase of the productive capacity may exert either expansive or depressing effects, depending on expectations, as already discussed in subsection 7.1.1, 7.3.1:

During the further phase the stabilizing policy may be challenged also by progresses in the developed country. Increases in the productivity of either labor or capital in the consumption goods sector requires an intensification of the stabilizing intervention (16.15) because their expansive effects now show up in an increase of imports which worsens their perturbative effects[7].

---

[5] Compare formulae (16.1) and (16.2).

[6] Compare (16.22) and (16.20).

[7] In subsection 16.5.1 we have shown that this is not the case during the early phase because of productive capacity constraints in the small country. This is reflected in the invariance of the right hand side of (15.22) with respect to l_1, b_1, l_2, b_2.

17 Remarks and Open Problems

17.1 Fiscal policy of the developed country and expansion of the new industrial sector in the developing country

In this part we have described how an export oriented sector may arise and develop in an underdeveloped country, possibly as the result of a deliberate political choice of the local government. We have assumed that the export flow is directed towards a large advanced country whence the productive technology and the respective instrumental goods are imported.

We have described the perturbations induced by this industrialization process in the economy of the developed country and we have proved that its government may implement effective stabilization policies both in the early phase and in the further one, if any. Assuming that the government does so, the demand for imported goods in the large country allows the new sector to survive and its development depend on its relative profitability with respect to the competitor sector in the large country.

If the profitability is sufficiently high a catching up process begins, otherwise the relative size of the new sector with respect to the competitor falls. In the first case the marked share of the new sector stabilizes, while it declines in the second case.

17.2 Fiscal policy of the developed country, budget and trade balance deficit

It is to be stressed that a budget deficit is required for the effectiveness of the stabilization policy; absolute value of the deficit is not high, since it is proportional to the (small) size of the modern sector (see (15.22) and (16.15)); however it is systematic and can not be maintained for ever. Moreover it is easy to see that the trade balance of the developed country is in deficit too, because the value of exported capital goods is less than the value of imported consumption goods during both the early and the further phase[1].

This rises problems in the medium long run, but these difficulties must not be overestimated. First of all the initial capital stock installed in the new modern sector has necessarily been purchased on credit, since the backward sector is unable to generate a flow of export competing on foreign markets. Thus the surplus of the trade balance of the small country is necessary for the debt service, at least in the early phase[2]. Second, the persistence of the trade balance deficit along the whole further phase depends on the assumption that modern and traditional sectors in the small country are completely separated; this is surely a good approximation in the early phase and at the beginning of the further one, but needs to be relaxed as the industrialization process in the small country has to continue.

The diffusion of the new imported technology can not let the traditional sector unaffected for ever; it is natural to assume that, after the successful growth of the modern sectors and the connected development of skills and externalities characterizing a more advanced context, also firms in the traditional sector start a restructuring process and begin importing modern capital goods.

Analogous considerations apply to the assumption that workers in the small country demand only goods produced by the domestic traditional sector. The developing of the modern sector is bound to increase per capita income and diffuse new standards of life. Thus it is reasonable to assume that during the further phase an increasing demand for imported consumption goods will arise from workers of both sectors of the small country.

---

[1]Deficit and surplus in the trade balances are bound to generate capital movements in the opposite direction. Since we are assuming (see subsection 13.3.2) that the start of the industrialization process is favored by an act of deliberate policy of the government of the underdeveloped country that participate to the repayment of the initial debt, a flow of capital from the small to the large country is nothing but the flow of instalments through which the repayment takes place.

[2]For a more detailed discussion of the problem of the debt burden faced by a developing country we refer again to Cantalupi Nardini and Ricottilli (1992) and the references cited there.

It is clear that, if this is the case, the resulting increase of the demand for consumption goods in the large country allow the government to reduce and eventually cancel outlays aimed at expanding the internal demand. It is even possible that the expansion of the demand begins fueling inflation forcing the government to implement anti-inflationary policies; in this case a budget surplus arises that allows the government to reduce the outstanding debt.

Moreover, the increase of exports of capital and consumption goods will progressively cancel the deficit of the trade balance and may revert it to a surplus. Obviously an analytic description of these further developments would require another extension of our model in order to include also the traditional sector of the small country. This extension, albeit possible, is beyond the scope of the present work.

18 Conclusions

The main purpose of this work has been to analyze the stability of equilibrium of a capitalist economy. We have considered the different regimes that characterize its working: normal equilibrium, overheating and depression, the effects of technical progress on equilibrium positions and on the dynamics far from equilibrium, the possibility and effectiveness of different types of fiscal policies.

The problem of equilibrium has been dealt with, at the analytical level, in terms of a four dimensional deterministic dynamical system framed in continuous time with the degree of capacity utilization of the consumption goods sector, the stock of inventories of the consumption goods sector, the relative price of commodities and the structure of the fixed capital stocks as state variables.

The dynamical system has a continuum of equilibrium points $(\bar{u}, \bar{s}, \bar{p}, \bar{z})$ where $\bar{u}, \bar{s}$ characterize the normal equilibrium in real terms and $\bar{p} = \Psi(\bar{z})$. From the analytical point of view the existence of a continuum of equilibria depends on the fact that quantities do not react directly on prices.

From the economic point of view the normal equilibrium of the model exhibits the usual properties of such a configuration of the economy: productive capacity of the sectors is utilized at the normal level, stocks of inventories are at their normal level and prices of commodities are constant, i.e. there is no inflation.

The existence of a one dimensional manifold of equilibria is perhaps unusual but far from been surprising as the effects of disproportions among sectors can be balanced by a suitable price structure, at least within given bounds. These bounds can not be overcome without undermining profit and growth rates of some sectors, together with the equilibrium of the system as a whole.

The stability analysis shows that the normal equilibrium is (locally) asymptotically unstable; the economy can evolve, therefore, according to two different regimes. The first regime is what we call expansion; its main features are a stock of inventories that diminish continuously in time, an increasing degree of capacity utilization and a relative price continuously increasing. The second regime is what we call depression; its characteristics are a rising level of inventories, falling prices of consumption goods and a decreasing degree of capacity utilization.

Let us consider the case of depression. The model shows that as the economy stays in such a regime for a sufficiently long time then an increasing disproportions between sectors arises that makes investment in the capital goods sector less and less profitable. In other words we have that the reduction of investments in the consumption goods sector determines an over-dimensioned capital goods sector; the excess of productive capacity that, in fact, characterizes the capital goods sector will eventually bring to a halt the accumulation process.

Things are the other way around in the case of the expansion regime. The increasing relative price causes a redistribution of profits in favor of the consumption goods sector; the disequilibrium among sectors grows steadily and ultimately leads the economy to an overheating phase. The consequence of this is either the rationing of the capital goods sector or the arrest of accumulation due to a lack of profits.

Thus the steady state growth trend is superimposed a cyclical irregular dynamics and its turning points represent true crisis phases of the economic system. Moreover these oscillations are by no means damped, nor their persistence depends on exogenous perturbations such as waves of optimism and pessimism, monetary and government policies, changes in technology and productivity, shifts in foreign demand and supply.

Obviously all these phenomena may prime the oscillation as shown in chapters 7 15 16, but their persistence is completely endogenous and has to be traced back to intertemporal coordination failures among different sectors, due to the length of productive fixed capital accumulation process: "the existence of an inherited stock of fixed capital goods implies a structural barrier to short term responses"[1] when changes in the demand occur.

In this scenario the effects of technical progress is not unambiguous. In general, productivity increases in one sector either rise the profit rate of one or both sectors, or allow longer expansion phases and less severe depressions. If this is the case the growth rate of the system rises and the economy will experience an expansion which may drive it to an overheating. However it may happen that the unexpected availability of a larger productive

---

[1] See Hagemann and Gehrke (1996).

capacity causes involuntary stockpiling and eventually an overproduction crisis. This undesirable outcome can be avoided if the innovation generates an expectation of a faster growth requiring higher investment in both sectors. We want to underline that technical progress may cause demand to recover at the deepest point of the depression; thus our model allows for exogenous causes for recoveries as well.

The element of innovation and technological transition (*exogenous* stimuli) gives the economic expansion, furthermore, a feature of unpredictability with regards to its timing, duration, and depth[2]. The role of innovation and technical change in priming an upswing is clearly recognized in the structural theories of the business cycle[3].

A quite natural question in this context is whether the government can step in and drive the economy to an equilibrium with higher growth rate, avoiding both overheating and depression. In the third part we tried to answer to this question: we have investigated the effectiveness of some fiscal policies aimed at stabilizing a capitalist economy that may move from an equilibrium position toward either an overheating or a depression phase.

In our model the government may prevent the overheating issuing new taxes: two conditions are crucial for the effectiveness of this strategy.

The additional revenue of these taxes must be used to increase government budget surplus; if the revenue is either spent on the consumption goods market or devoted to direct transfers to households, the demand is simply shifted, but not reduced and the overheating can not be avoided..

The taxes that allow to prevent the overheating are either consumption taxes or profit taxes. Consumption taxes reduce the demand for consumption goods, but they indirectly reduce the demand for capital goods too, since they lower profits and investment in the consumption goods sector.

Profit taxes have a somewhat different effect: they reduce net profit and investment in both sectors on the one side; on the other side the demand for consumption goods is reduced both directly and indirectly, via a reduction of the demand for capital goods that lowers the activity level of that sector. However a problem of compatibility arises because the profit taxation is stabilizing only if the tax rate is sufficiently high, on the other hand the tax rate can not overcome an upper bound over which profitability and investment is undermined in at least one sector. In such circumstances the disproportion between sectors increases and the equilibrium is lost.

The strategies to prevent depressions are in some sense symmetric: they may consist in either tax cuts or increases of direct transfers.

In this case these interventions are effective provided that they are financed by deficit spending. Should the cut be balanced by a parallel re-

---

[2] See Hagemann and Landesmann (1998).

[3] See in particular Tugan-Baranowskj (1901), Bouniatin (1922), Spiethoff (1925), Hicks (1973), Lowe (1976).

duction of government spending, the expansionary effects would be lost because of an induced reduction of the aggregate demand.

Moreover consumption tax cuts cause a direct increase of the demand for consumption goods and an indirect increase of the demand for capital goods due to the rise of profitability of both sectors.

Also a reduction of profit taxes may exert growth effects priming a recovery of consumption goods demand, provided it is sufficiently large. Again this may be impossible to achieve since the initial profit tax can not overcome some threshold without destroying the equilibrium of the economy.

As far as an increase of direct transfers is concerned, they are effective provided that they are in some sense proportional to the number of workers who have lost their jobs because of the depression[4]. However issuing unemployment benefits for structurally unemployed workers financed by deficit spending would be not only ineffective to prevent oscillations, but would even destroy the equilibria of the system.

The case of an open economy obviously entails a substantial revision of the model and possibly severe perturbations of the equilibrium positions. The government of a single country is hardly able to stabilize the economy of its own country by unilateral interventions, unless the country is sufficiently "large" with respect to the others.

In part four we have treated precisely this case: a large developed country faces the industrialization process of a small underdeveloped one. The government of the large country can still stabilize the economy, provided the stabilizing policies described in the third part are suitably adapted, since now they must at a time contrast the internal instability factors and the perturbations induced by the import export flows.

If the stabilization policies implemented by the government of the large country work correctly for a sufficiently long time after the beginning of the industrialization of the small one and the accumulated profit in the new modern sector is large enough, a catching up process takes place and the modern sector grows quickly, fueled by a stable foreign demand.

There is a further problem arising in the open economy case: the stabilizing fiscal policies may entail a moderate but persistent budget deficit together with a deficit in the trade balance of the large country. The possibility of reducing these deficits and eventually revert them into surpluses is beyond the government action and depends on the evolution of the industrialization process in the small country.

---

[4]This may be rephrased as follows: the increase of direct transfers must compensate the fall of the aggregate demand caused by the depression.

"Another case of demand picking up would be...export demand which could also be generated through credit links 'this type of demand is often based on export credits granted by the exporting country (Bouniatin 1922 p. 252)", see Hagemann and Landeasmann (1998).

Last but not least, the beginning of the industrialization process in the underdeveloped country may stimulate the economy of the advanced one to overcome a slump, thus providing a third[5] exogenous source of additional growth. The complex interplay of endogenous and exogenous factors characterizing our model leads to a business cycle in which timing and strength of the different phases are hardly foreseeable and industrial fluctuations follows irregular and complex patterns. On the other hand the government of the large country can considerably dampen fluctuations with proper fiscal policies.

---

[5] After technical progress and government interventions discussed above.

19 Appendices

19.1 Appendix 1. Profit rates in the two sectors.

In this appendix we calculate the profit rates r_1 and r_2 in both sectors.

19.1.1 The consumption goods sector

The ratio between the difference (3.5) between the value of the total output (3.1) and production costs in the first sector and the total capital (3.14) engaged in production is

$$r_1 = \frac{Y_1 p_1 - W_1 - \delta K_1 p_2}{C_1}. \tag{19.1}$$

Substituting from (3.4), (3.15), (3.15), and (4.1) we obtain

$$r_1 = \frac{(b_1 - wl_1)p_1 u - \delta}{k_1}. \tag{19.2}$$

Having in mind (4.6) and (4.7), equation (19.2) becomes

$$r_1 = b_1 \beta u - \frac{\delta}{k_1}. \tag{19.3}$$

In a normal equilibrium (19.3) becomes

$$\bar{r}_1 = b_1 \bar{\beta} \bar{u} - \frac{\delta}{k_1}. \tag{19.4}$$

19.1.2   The capital goods sector

The analogous of the rate (19.1) for firms in the capital goods sector is

$$r_2 = \frac{Y_2 p_2 - W_2 - \delta K_2 p_2}{K_1 p_2} \tag{19.5}$$

Again substituting from (3.1), (3.20), and (4.1) we obtain

$$r_2 = \frac{Y_2}{K_2}\left(1 - \frac{wl_2}{b_2}p\right) - \delta. \tag{19.6}$$

We complete the computation substituting from (4.16) and (4.17) into (19.6); after obvious simplifications we obtain

$$r_2 = b_1 \beta u h(u) + (d_1 + \delta) h(u)\frac{k_1 - 1}{k_1} + d_1\left(\frac{b_2}{wl_2 p} - 1\right)(h(u) - 1). \tag{19.7}$$

In every normal equilibrium point (3.1), equation (A-6) reads

$$\overline{r}_2 = b_1 \overline{\beta}\overline{u} - \frac{1}{k_1}\delta + d_1\frac{\overline{k}_1 - 1}{\overline{k}_1} \tag{19.8}$$

Comparing (19.4) and (19.8) it is clear that in those equilibrium points the rate of profit in the capital goods sector is higher than in the consumption goods sector; the gap between the two rates decreases when the normal inventory level in the consumption goods sector decreases.

19.2   Appendix 2. Growth rate of the economy

The growth rate ρ of the consumption goods sector (4.10) equals the one of the capital goods sector in every normal equilibrium point (5.1); this can be easily proved substituting the right hand sides of equations (4.16) and (5.1) into (3.3).

We denote the common value by $\overline{\rho}$ and define it growth rate of the system in equilibrium; its value is

$$\overline{\rho} = \frac{(b_1 - wl_1)\overline{pu} - (\delta + d_1)}{k_1} \tag{19.9}$$

It is clear that $\overline{\rho}$ is an increasing function with respect to the equilibrium relative price $\overline{p}$ and to the normal capacity utilization rate $\overline{u}$, whereas it is decreasing with respect to the normal inventory level $\overline{s}$, if $\overline{\rho} > 0$, while it is increasing if this is not the case; however this second case does not occur if condition (5.5) holds, as we have assumed.

19.3   Appendix 3. Instability of normal equilibria

In this appendix we give a proof of theorem 1.

19.3.1   Linearization of the non-linear system (4.29)

Simple calculations yield the following Jacobian matrix of the linearized system, evaluated at one of the equilibrium points $\bar{\eta} = (\bar{u}, \bar{s}, \bar{p}, \bar{z})(5.1)$

$$
J = \begin{bmatrix}
\dfrac{\partial F(\bar{\eta})}{\partial u} & \dfrac{\partial F(\bar{\eta})}{\partial s} & 0 & 0 \\[2mm]
-\dfrac{\bar{k}}{\bar{p}b_1}\left(\bar{\alpha}+b_1\bar{\beta}\bar{u}\right)\bar{h}' & 0 & 0 & 0 \\[2mm]
0 & \bar{p}\bar{g}_1' & 0 & 0 \\[2mm]
\dfrac{\partial H(\bar{\eta})}{\partial u} & \dfrac{\partial H(\bar{\eta})}{\partial s} & \dfrac{\partial H(\bar{\eta})}{\partial p} & \dfrac{\partial H(\bar{\eta})}{\partial z}
\end{bmatrix} \tag{19.10}
$$

To determine the eigenvalues of the Jacobian matrix J it is sufficient to write the explicit expression of the last partial derivative of the function H in the equilibrium point

$$
\frac{\partial H(\bar{\eta})}{\partial z} = -\left(\bar{\alpha}+b_1\bar{\beta}\bar{u}+\frac{d_2 b_2}{w l_2 \bar{p}}\right). \tag{19.11}
$$

19.3.2   Characteristic polynomial

Hence the characteristic polynomial of the linearized system is

$$
\begin{aligned}
P(\lambda) \;=\; & \lambda\left(\bar{\alpha}+b_1\bar{\beta}\bar{u}+\frac{d_2 b_2}{w l_2 \bar{p}}+\lambda\right) \\
& \left(\lambda^2 - \frac{\partial F(\bar{\eta})}{\partial u}\lambda + \frac{\bar{k}}{b_1\bar{p}}\frac{\partial F(\bar{\eta})}{\partial s}\left(\bar{\alpha}+b_1\bar{\beta}\bar{u}\right)\bar{h}'\right)
\end{aligned} \tag{19.12}
$$

In (19.10) and (19.11) the upper bar means that the function is calculated in the equilibrium point $\bar{\eta} = (\bar{u}, \bar{s}, \bar{p}, \bar{z})$.

19.3.3   Eigenvalues

The eigenvalues of the linearized system are:

$$
\lambda_1 = \frac{1}{2}\left(\frac{\partial F(\bar{\eta})}{\partial u} - \sqrt{\left(\frac{\partial F(\bar{\eta})}{\partial u}\right)^2 - 4\frac{\bar{k}}{b_1\bar{p}}\frac{\partial F(\bar{\eta})}{\partial s}\left(\bar{\alpha}+b_1\bar{\beta}\bar{u}\right)\bar{h}'}\right)
$$

$$
\lambda_2 = \frac{1}{2}\left(\frac{\partial F(\bar{\eta})}{\partial u} + \sqrt{\left(\frac{\partial F(\bar{\eta})}{\partial u}\right)^2 - 4\frac{\bar{k}}{b_1\bar{p}}\frac{\partial F(\bar{\eta})}{\partial s}\left(\bar{\alpha}+b_1\bar{\beta}\bar{u}\right)\bar{h}'}\right)
$$

$$\lambda_3 = 0 \tag{19.13}$$

$$\lambda_4 = -\left(\bar{\alpha} + b_1\bar{\beta}\bar{u} + \frac{d_2 b_2}{w l_2 \bar{p}}\right)$$

Hence, having in mind the hypotheses (3.16) on the sign of the partial derivatives of the function F, we have $\lambda_1 < 0$, $\lambda_4 < 0$, $\lambda_3 = 0$ and $\lambda_2 > 0$. All equilibria are therefore unstable.

19.4   Appendix 4. Dynamics near normal equilibria

19.4.1   Diagonalization and principal coordinates

To apply the adiabatic principle it is necessary to diagonalize the Jacobian matrix J; we thus introduce the matrix $\widehat{B}$ defined by:

$$\widehat{B} = (v_1, v_2, v_3, v_4) \tag{19.14}$$

where v_i $(i = 1, \ldots, 4)$ are the eigenvectors of the matrix of the linearized system:

$$v_1 = \begin{pmatrix} \dfrac{\partial F(\bar{\eta})}{\partial s} \\[4pt] \lambda_1 - \dfrac{\partial F(\bar{\eta})}{\partial u} \\[4pt] \dfrac{\bar{p}\bar{g}_1'}{\lambda_1}\left(\lambda_1 - \dfrac{\partial F(\bar{\eta})}{\partial u}\right) \\[6pt] \dfrac{\partial H(\bar{\eta})}{\partial p}\dfrac{\bar{p}\bar{g}_1'}{\lambda_1}\left(\lambda_1 - \dfrac{\partial F(\bar{\eta})}{\partial u}\right) \\[6pt] \bar{\alpha} + b_1\bar{\beta}\bar{u} + \dfrac{d_2 b_2}{w l_2 \bar{p}} + \lambda_1 \end{pmatrix} \qquad v_2 = \begin{pmatrix} \dfrac{\partial F(\bar{\eta})}{\partial s} \\[4pt] \lambda_2 - \dfrac{\partial F(\bar{\eta})}{\partial u} \\[4pt] \dfrac{\bar{p}\bar{g}_1'}{\lambda_2}\left(\lambda_2 - \dfrac{\partial F(\bar{\eta})}{\partial u}\right) \\[6pt] \dfrac{\partial H(\bar{\eta})}{\partial p}\dfrac{\bar{p}\bar{g}_1'}{\lambda_2}\left(\lambda_2 - \dfrac{\partial F(\bar{\eta})}{\partial u}\right) \\[6pt] \bar{\alpha} + b_1\bar{\beta}\bar{u} + \dfrac{d_2 b_2}{w l_2 \bar{p}} + \lambda_2 \end{pmatrix}$$

$$\tag{19.15}$$

$$v_3 = \begin{pmatrix} 0 \\ 0 \\ \bar{\alpha} + b_1\bar{\beta}\bar{u} + \dfrac{d_2 b_2}{w l_2 \bar{p}} \\[6pt] \dfrac{\partial H(\bar{\eta})}{\partial p} \end{pmatrix} \qquad v_4 = \begin{pmatrix} 0 \\ 0 \\ 0 \\ 1 \end{pmatrix}$$

Thus we have $\widehat{B}^{-1} J \widehat{B} = diag(\lambda_i)$ $(i = 1, \ldots, 4)$.
We introduce the new variables[1]:

$$x = \widehat{B}^{-1}(\eta - \bar{\eta}) \tag{19.16}$$

---

[1] These are analogous to the principal coordinates of [35]

where $x = (x_1, x_2, x_3, x_4)$ and $(\eta - \bar{\eta}) = (u - \bar{u}, s - \bar{s}, p - \bar{p}, z - \bar{z})$, i.e.

$$u - \bar{u} = \frac{\partial F(\bar{\eta})}{\partial s} x_1 + \frac{\partial F(\bar{\eta})}{\partial s} x_2 \tag{19.17}$$

$$s - \bar{s} = -\lambda_2 x_1 - \lambda_1 x_2$$

$$p - \bar{p} = -\frac{\lambda_2}{\lambda_1} \bar{p} \bar{g}_1' x_1 - \frac{\lambda_1}{\lambda_2} \bar{p} \bar{g}_1' x_2 + \left(\bar{\alpha} + b_1 \bar{\beta} \bar{u} + \frac{d_2 b_2}{w l_2 \bar{p}} \right) x_3$$

$$z - \bar{z} = -\frac{\partial H(\bar{\eta})}{\partial p} \frac{\bar{p} \bar{g}_1'}{\bar{\alpha} + b_1 \bar{\beta} \bar{u} + \frac{d_2 b_2}{w l_2 \bar{p}}} \left(\frac{\lambda_2}{\lambda_1} x_1 + \frac{\lambda_1}{\lambda_2} x_2 \right) + \frac{\partial H(\bar{\eta})}{\partial p} x_3 + x_4$$

19.4.2 Adiabatic approximation

In the new coordinate system the axes x_1 and x_4 are the two eigenspaces corresponding to the negative eigenvalues; hence, by the adiabatic principle, we may approximate the solution of the dynamical system (4.29) by setting:

$$\begin{cases} \dot{x}_1 = 0 \\ \dot{x}_4 = 0 \end{cases} \tag{19.18}$$

Deriving both members of (19.17) and using (19.18) we obtain

$$\begin{cases} \dot{u} = \dfrac{\partial F(\bar{\eta})}{\partial s} \dot{x}_2 \\[2mm] \dot{s} = -\lambda_1 \dot{x}_2 \\[2mm] \dot{p} = -\dfrac{\lambda_1}{\lambda_2} \bar{p} \bar{g}_1' \dot{x}_2 + \left(\bar{\alpha} + b_1 \bar{\beta} \bar{u} + \dfrac{d_2 b_2}{w l_2 \bar{p}} \right) \dot{x}_3 \\[4mm] \dot{z} = -\dfrac{\partial H(\bar{\eta})}{\partial p} \dfrac{\bar{p} \bar{g}_1'}{\bar{\alpha} + b_1 \bar{\beta} \bar{u} + \dfrac{d_2 b_2}{w l_2 \bar{p}}} \dfrac{\lambda_1}{\lambda_2} \dot{x}_2 + \dfrac{\partial H(\bar{\eta})}{\partial p} \dot{x}_3 \end{cases} \tag{19.19}$$

Now we eliminate x_2' and x_3' from (19.19); then using the notation introduced in (4.30) and (4.31), we obtain

$$\begin{cases} F(u, s) + \dfrac{\partial F(\bar{\eta})}{\partial s} + \dfrac{1}{\lambda_1} G(u, s, p) = 0 \\[4mm] z = -\dfrac{\partial H(\bar{\eta})}{\partial p} \dfrac{1}{\bar{\alpha} + b_1 \bar{\beta} \bar{u} + \dfrac{d_2 b_2}{w l_2 \bar{p}}} \dfrac{g_1(s) p}{(\alpha + b_1 \beta u) h(u) + \dfrac{d_2 b_2}{w l_2 p}} \\[6mm] \qquad + \dfrac{(\alpha + b_1 \beta u) h(u)}{(\alpha + b_1 \beta u) h(u) + \dfrac{d_2 b_2}{w l_2 p}} \left(\dfrac{b_2}{w l_2 p} - 1 \right) \end{cases} \tag{19.20}$$

After obvious simplifications we obtain the required expression (5.15).

19.5   Appendix 5. Proof of (5.14) and (5.15)

Equations (4.29) and (19.14) immediately imply the second and third equations in (5.14), since the two functions $u(t)$ and $s(t)$ are decreasing and increasing respectively.

19.5.1   Proof of (5.14)

The proof of the first equation in (5.14) can be obtained showing that the function $t \to s(t)p(t)$ is decreasing: namely

$$\frac{d}{dt}(s(t)p(t)) = \left[\delta p(t)s(t) + \left(1 - \frac{wl_1}{b_1}\right)p(t)u(t) - \frac{d_1}{b_1}\right] \quad (19.21)$$
$$(h(u(t)) - 1) + s(t)g_1(s(t))p(t),$$

moreover, when $u(t) < \bar{u}$ and $s(t) > \bar{s}$, both terms in the right hand side of (19.21) are negative.

Hence there exists the limit $\lim\limits_{t \to \hat{t}-} s(t)p(t)$ and it may be either positive or zero. We conclude the proof showing that only the first alternative may occur. In fact, assume that the limit is zero, then we consider the limit

$$\lim_{t \to \hat{t}-} \frac{\dot{s}(t)}{\frac{1}{(p(t))^2}\dot{p}(t)} \frac{d_1}{b_1} = \quad (19.22)$$

$$\lim_{t \to \hat{t}-} \frac{(1 - h(u(t)))p(t)}{g_1(s(t))}$$

$$\left(\left(1 - \frac{wl_1}{b_1}\right)p(t)u(t) + \delta p(t)s(t) - \frac{d_1}{b_1}\right);$$

taking into account that

$$\lim_{t \to \hat{t}-} s(t)p(t) = \lim_{t \to \hat{t}-} \frac{s(t)}{\frac{1}{p(t)}}, \quad (19.23)$$

if $\lim\limits_{t \to \hat{t}-} s(t)p(t) \in R^+$ the numerator of the right hand side of (19.22) has a finite limit as t converges to $\hat{t}$ from below , whereas the denominator diverges, whence a contradiction.

19.6   Appendix 6. Proof of (5.11) and (5.13)

From formulas (4.29) and (19.14) we easily deduce that the capacity utilization rate u is an increasing function, while the inventory level s is a decreasing one; thus there exists a finite or infinite $\tilde{t}$ such that the second and third equations (5.11) hold. On the other hand, as $\lim\limits_{s\to 0+} sg_1(s) = +\infty$, it is easy to prove, using (19.21), that the derivative $\frac{d}{dt}s(t)p(t)$ is positive for t in a suitable left neighborhood of $\tilde{t}$; hence the function $t \to s(t)p(t)$ is increasing there and this is sufficient to prove the first equation in (5.11).

The proof of (5.13) is obtained by contradiction too. We begin observing that, if

$\lim\limits_{t\to\tilde{t}-} s(t)p(t) \in R^+$, then it is easy to see that the right hand side of (19.22) diverges to $+\infty$ as t converges to $\tilde{t}$ from the left; this leads to a contradiction.

19.7 Appendix 7. Proof of theorems in Chapter 6

19.7.1 Proof of (6.1)

Conditions (5.14) and (5.15) yield

$$\lim_{t\to\hat{t}-} k(t) = 1$$
$$\lim_{t\to\hat{t}-} \alpha(t) = -d_1 \qquad (19.24)$$
$$\lim_{t\to\hat{t}-} \beta(t) = 0$$

Moreover, if $I_2(t) > 0$ held for every $t > 0$, then condition (4.21) would hold and hence both $I_1(t) > 0$ and $z(t) > 0$ would hold for every $t > 0$, since (4.21) implies (4.20). So in this hypothesis the left hand side of (4.21) would be positive for every $t > 0$.

On the other hand

$$\lim_{t\to\hat{t}-} \alpha(t) + b_1\beta(t) = -d_1 \qquad (19.25)$$

and thus the right hand side of (4.21) would become zero at least in a point t_a ; this would mean that $I_2(t_a) = 0$, again by (4.21). Whence the contradiction.

19.7.2 Proof of theorem 4

Assume by contradiction that $\dot{p}(t) > 0$ for every $t > \tilde{t}$; then there exists an instant $\tilde{t}_a \in [\tilde{t}_0, \tilde{t}]$ such that $\dot{z}(t) < 0$ for $t > \tilde{t}_a$, whence $\lim\limits_{t\to\tilde{t}-} z(t) = 0$.

Therefore we immediately have

$$\lim_{t\to\tilde{t}-} \frac{(\alpha(t) + b_1\beta(t))\,h\,(u(t))}{b_2} \frac{1}{z(t)} - \frac{wl_2p(t) + d_2}{b_2} = +\infty \qquad (19.26)$$

Conditions (3.8) and (3.30) on the dynamics of prices p_1 and p_2 and in particular $\lim\limits_{s\to 0+} g_1(s) = +\infty$ together with $\lim\limits_{s\to +\infty} g_2(s) = -\infty$ lead to a contradiction.

19.8   Appendix 8. Existence of an overheating stationary equilibrium

The condition $\mathcal{H}^\nabla\left(\overline{p^\nabla}, \overline{z^\nabla}\right) = 0$ there exists a trade-off between the relative price $\overline{p^\nabla}$ and the relative fixed capital stock $\overline{z^\nabla}$ at such equilibrium point

$$\overline{z^\nabla} = \frac{b_2 - wl_2\overline{p^\nabla} - d_2}{wl_2\overline{p^\nabla} + d_2} \tag{19.27}$$

Analogously, the condition $\mathcal{G}^\nabla\left(\overline{u^\nabla}, \overline{s^\nabla}, \overline{p^\nabla}, \overline{z^\nabla}\right) = 0$ yields a second relation

$$\overline{z^\nabla} = \frac{(b_1 - wl_1)\,\overline{u^\nabla p^\nabla} + \delta b_1 \overline{s^\nabla p^\nabla} - d_1}{\left(b_1\overline{s^\nabla p^\nabla} + 1\right)\left(wl_2\overline{p^\nabla} + d_2\right)} \tag{19.28}$$

Now we equate the right hand sides of (19.27) and (19.28) and obtain

$$(b_1 - wl_1)\overline{u^\nabla p^\nabla} + \delta b_1\overline{s^\nabla p^\nabla} - d_1 = \left(b_1\overline{s^\nabla p^\nabla} + 1\right)\left(b_2 - wl_2\overline{p^\nabla} - d_2\right) \tag{19.29}$$

By substituting (19.28) into (4.62), the equation $\mathcal{K}\left(\overline{u^\nabla}, \overline{s^\nabla}, \overline{p^\nabla}, \overline{z^\nabla}\right) = 0$ becomes

$$g_1\left(\overline{s^\nabla}\right) = g_2\left(\frac{wl_2\overline{p^\nabla} + d_2}{b_2}\left(h\left(\overline{u^\nabla}\right) - 1\right)\right); \tag{19.30}$$

using again the above conditions (19.29) (19.30) together with $F\left(\overline{u^\nabla}, \overline{s^\nabla}\right) = 0$ we obtain the equilibrium values $\overline{u^\nabla}$, $\overline{s^\nabla}$, and $\overline{p^\nabla}$; we get, in particular

$$\overline{s^\nabla} = \frac{(b_1 - wl_1)\,\overline{u^\nabla}, \overline{p^\nabla} - \left(b_2 - wl_2\overline{p^\nabla}\right)}{\left(b_2 - wl_2\overline{p^\nabla} - d_2 - \delta\right)} \tag{19.31}$$

It is easy to prove that a solution of the system formed by (19.31) and $\mathcal{F}^\nabla\left(\overline{u^\nabla}, \overline{s^\nabla}\right) = 0$

$$\begin{cases} \overline{s^\nabla} = \dfrac{(b_1 - wl_1)\,\overline{u^\nabla}, \overline{p^\nabla} - \left(b_2 - wl_2\overline{p^\nabla}\right)}{\left(b_2 - wl_2\overline{p^\nabla} - d_2 - \delta\right)} \\ F\left(\bar{u}^*, \bar{s}^*\right) = 0 \end{cases} \tag{19.32}$$

exists for every $\overline{p^\nabla}$ such that

$$\overline{p^\nabla} \geq \frac{b_2}{(b_1 - wl_1)\,\tilde{u} + wl_2}, \tag{19.33}$$

if[2]

$$\tilde{u} > \frac{(d_1 + \delta)\,wl_2}{(b_1 - wl_1)(b_2 - d_2 - \delta)}. \tag{19.34}$$

(19.34) is precisely (6.4).

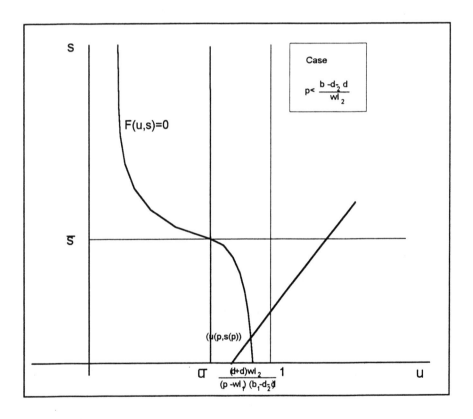

FIGURE 19.1. projection of the overheating equilibrium on the $u - s$ plane

---

[2] See 19.1 .

19.9 Appendix 9. Stability of the overheating stationary equilibrium

Here we study the stability of the overheating stationary equilibrium

$$\left(\overline{u^\nabla}, \overline{s^\nabla}, \overline{p^\nabla}, \overline{z^\nabla}\right),$$

whenever it exists.

19.9.1 Linearization of the non-linear system (4.60)

To this aim we compute the Jacobian matrix $\overline{J^\nabla}$ of the system in the equilibrium point $\left(\overline{u^\nabla}, \overline{s^\nabla}, \overline{p^\nabla}, \overline{z^\nabla}\right)$, having in mind the relations (19.27), (19.30), (19.31), and (19.32) linking the coordinates of this point

$$\overline{J^\nabla} = \qquad\qquad (19.35)$$

$$
\begin{bmatrix}
\dfrac{\partial \overline{F^\nabla}}{\partial u} \cdot & \dfrac{\partial \overline{F^\nabla}}{\partial s} & 0 & 0 \\[2ex]
\left(1 - \dfrac{wl_1}{b_1}\right) & b_2 - wl_2\overline{p^\nabla} - d_2 - \delta & \dfrac{d_1}{b_1\overline{p^\nabla}} - wl_2\overline{s^\nabla}\,\overline{z^\nabla} & \dfrac{wl_2\overline{p^\nabla} + d_2}{b_1\overline{p^\nabla}}\left(b_1\overline{p^\nabla}\,\overline{s^\nabla} + 1\right) \\[2ex]
\dfrac{\partial \overline{K^\nabla}}{\partial u}\overline{p^\nabla} & \dfrac{\partial \overline{K^\nabla}}{\partial s}\overline{p^\nabla} & \dfrac{\partial \overline{K^\nabla}}{\partial p}\overline{p^\nabla} & \dfrac{\partial \overline{K^\nabla}}{\partial z}\overline{p^\nabla} \\[2ex]
0 & 0 & -wl_2\left(\overline{z^\nabla} + \overline{z^\nabla}^2\right) & -\left(b_2 - wl_2\overline{p^\nabla} - d_2 - \delta\right)
\end{bmatrix}
$$

19.9.2 Characteristic polynomial

It is easy to see that the roots of the corresponding characteristic polynomial $\overline{P^\nabla}(\lambda)$ obviously depend on the explicit expression of the derivatives appearing in the third row of the matrix $\overline{J^\nabla}$ (19.35); for instance, if we assume that at the equilibrium point both functions g_1 and g_2 are stationary, then the third row is null and the characteristic polynomial becomes

$$\overline{P^\nabla}(\lambda) = \qquad\qquad (19.36)$$
$$\left[\lambda^2 + \left(b_2 - wl_2\overline{p^\nabla} - d_2 - \delta - \dfrac{\partial \overline{F^\nabla}}{\partial u}\right)\lambda - \dfrac{\partial \overline{F^\nabla}}{\partial s}\left(1 - \dfrac{wl_1}{b_1}\right)\right]$$
$$\lambda\left(b_2 - wl_2\overline{p^\nabla} - d_2 - \delta + \lambda\right).$$

Among the roots of this polynomial one is obviously zero, another is negative and two of them have negative real part. Hence the stability of the equilibrium point depends crucially on the second derivatives.

Thus it is evident that the equilibrium point, whenever it exists, may be locally attractive .

19.10   Appendix 10. Proof of theorem 9

19.10.1   *Linearization and characteristic polynomial*

We start observing that $\frac{\partial G(\bar{\eta})}{\partial p} = 0$ in every equilibrium point $\bar{\eta} = (\bar{u}, \bar{s}, \bar{p}, \bar{z})$; thus the matrix of the linearized system in such equilibria is

$$
J = \begin{pmatrix}
\dfrac{\partial F(\bar{\eta})}{\partial u} & \dfrac{\partial F(\bar{\eta})}{\partial s} & 0 & 0 \\[2mm]
\dfrac{\partial G(\bar{\eta})}{\partial u} & \dfrac{\partial G(\bar{\eta})}{\partial s} & 0 & 0 \\[2mm]
0 & \bar{p}\bar{g}_1' & 0 & 0 \\[2mm]
\dfrac{\partial H(\bar{\eta})}{\partial u} & \dfrac{\partial H(\bar{\eta})}{\partial s} & \dfrac{\partial H(\bar{\eta})}{\partial p} & \dfrac{\partial H(\bar{\eta})}{\partial z}
\end{pmatrix}
\tag{19.37}
$$

Its eigenvalues are

$$
\lambda_3 = 0 \tag{19.38}
$$

$$
\lambda_4 = -\left(\bar{\alpha} + b_1\bar{\beta}\bar{u} + \frac{db_2}{wl_2\bar{p}}\right)
$$

and the two roots λ_1, λ_2 of the polynomial

$$
P_1(\lambda) = \lambda^2 - \left(\frac{\partial F(\bar{\eta})}{\partial u} + \frac{\partial G(\bar{\eta})}{\partial s}\right)\lambda + \frac{\partial F(\bar{\eta})}{\partial u}\frac{\partial G(\bar{\eta})}{\partial s} - \frac{\partial F(\bar{\eta})}{\partial s}\frac{\partial G(\bar{\eta})}{\partial u}
\tag{19.39}
$$

19.10.2   *Sign of the eigenvalues*

Since $\frac{\partial F(\bar{\eta})}{\partial s} < 0$ by our assumptions on output decisions in the consumption goods sector (see subsections 3.2.2 and 2.2.2).

$$
\frac{\partial G(\bar{\eta})}{\partial s} = \frac{\vartheta g_1'(\bar{s})}{1 - \bar{t}^c}\frac{1}{b_1\bar{p}}\left(wl_1\overline{pu} + (\bar{\alpha} + b_1\bar{\beta}\bar{u}) + d_1\right) < 0,
\tag{19.40}
$$

both roots of the polynomial (19.39) are negative (or have negative real part) if and only if

$$
\frac{\partial F(\bar{\eta})}{\partial u}\frac{\partial G(\bar{\eta})}{\partial s} - \frac{\partial F(\bar{\eta})}{\partial s}\frac{\partial G(\bar{\eta})}{\partial u} > 0.
\tag{19.41}
$$

This means

$$
-\frac{\partial F(\bar{\eta})}{\partial s}\frac{\bar{k}}{b_1\bar{p}}\left(\bar{\alpha} + b_1\bar{\beta}\bar{u}\right)h'(\bar{u}) \leqslant
\tag{19.42}
$$

$$
\frac{\partial F(\bar{\eta})}{\partial u}\frac{\vartheta g_1'(\bar{s})}{1 - \bar{t}^c}\frac{1}{b_1\bar{p}} \cdot
$$

$$
\left(wl_1\overline{pu} + (\bar{\alpha} + b_1\bar{\beta}\bar{u}) + d_1\right)
$$

whence

$$\vartheta > -\frac{\dfrac{\partial F\left(\bar{\eta}\right)}{\partial s}}{\dfrac{\partial F\left(\bar{\eta}\right)}{\partial u}}\frac{g_1'\left(\bar{s}\right)}{1-\bar{t}^c}\frac{\bar{k}\left(\bar{\alpha}+b_1\bar{\beta}\bar{u}\right)h'\left(\bar{u}\right)}{\left(wl_1\overline{pu}+\left(\bar{\alpha}+b_1\bar{\beta}\bar{u}\right)+d_1\right)} \tag{19.43}$$

Equation (19.43) is precisely (11.16).
This completes the proof of theorem 9.

19.11   Appendix 11. Proof of theorem 7

19.11.1   Linearization and characteristic polynomial

We start observing that

$$\frac{\partial G\left(\bar{\eta}\right)}{\partial s} = 0$$

$$\frac{\partial G\left(\bar{\eta}\right)}{\partial z} = 0$$

in the equilibrium point $\bar{\eta} = \left(\bar{u}, \bar{s}, \bar{p}, \bar{z}\right)$ given by (11.8) and (11.9); thus the matrix of the linearized system in such equilibrium is

$$J = \begin{pmatrix} \dfrac{\partial F\left(\bar{\eta}\right)}{\partial u} & \dfrac{\partial F\left(\bar{\eta}\right)}{\partial s} & 0 & 0 \\[2mm] \dfrac{\partial G\left(\bar{\eta}\right)}{\partial u} & 0 & \dfrac{\partial G\left(\bar{\eta}\right)}{\partial p} & 0 \\[2mm] 0 & \bar{p}g_1' & 0 & 0 \\[2mm] \dfrac{\partial H\left(\bar{\eta}\right)}{\partial u} & \dfrac{\partial H\left(\bar{\eta}\right)}{\partial s} & \dfrac{\partial H\left(\bar{\eta}\right)}{\partial p} & \dfrac{\partial H\left(\bar{\eta}\right)}{\partial z} \end{pmatrix} \tag{19.44}$$

Its eigenvalues are

$$\lambda_4 = -\left(\bar{\alpha}+b_1\bar{\beta}\bar{u}+\frac{db_2}{wl_2\bar{p}}\right) \tag{19.45}$$

and the three roots $\lambda_1, \lambda_2, \lambda_3$ of the polynomial

$$P_1\left(\lambda\right) = \lambda^3 - \frac{\partial F\left(\bar{\eta}\right)}{\partial u}\lambda^2 + \left(-\frac{\partial F\left(\bar{\eta}\right)}{\partial s}\frac{\partial G\left(\bar{\eta}\right)}{\partial u} - \right. \tag{19.46}$$
$$\left. g_1'\left(\bar{s}\right)\bar{p}\frac{\partial G\left(\bar{\eta}\right)}{\partial p}\right)\lambda + g_1'\left(\bar{s}\right)\bar{p}\frac{\partial G\left(\bar{\eta}\right)}{\partial p}\frac{\partial F\left(\bar{\eta}\right)}{\partial s}\frac{\partial G\left(\bar{\eta}\right)}{\partial u}$$

19.11.2 Sign of the eigenvalues

Since $\frac{\partial F(\bar{\eta})}{\partial s} < 0$ by our assumptions on output decisions in the consumption goods sector (see again subsection 3.2.2) and

$$\frac{\partial G(\bar{\eta})}{\partial p} = \frac{\bar{p}_2 \vartheta'(\bar{p}_1)}{1 - \bar{t}^c} \frac{1}{b_1 \bar{p}} \left(wl_1 \overline{pu} + (\bar{\alpha} + b_1 \overline{\beta u}) + d_1 \right) > 0 \quad (19.47)$$

$$\frac{\partial G(\bar{\eta})}{\partial u} = -\frac{k}{b_1 \bar{p}} (\bar{\alpha} + b_1 \overline{\beta u}) h'(\bar{u}) < 0,$$

all the roots of the polynomial (19.46) are negative (or have negative real part) if and only if

$$-\frac{\partial F(\bar{\eta})}{\partial s} \frac{\partial G(\bar{\eta})}{\partial u} - g_1'(\bar{s}) \bar{p} \frac{\partial G(\bar{\eta})}{\partial p} > 0. \quad (19.48)$$

This means

$$\frac{\partial F(\bar{\eta})}{\partial s} \frac{k}{b_1 \bar{p}} (\bar{\alpha} + b_1 \overline{\beta u}) h'(\bar{u}) \leqslant \quad (19.49)$$

$$g_1'(\bar{p}) \frac{\bar{p}_2 \vartheta'(\bar{p}_1)}{1 - \bar{t}^c} \frac{1}{b_1 \bar{p}} \cdot$$
$$\left(wl_1 \overline{pu} + (\bar{\alpha} + b_1 \overline{\beta u}) + d_1 \right)$$

whence

$$\vartheta'(\bar{p}_1) > \frac{1 - \bar{t}^c}{\bar{p}_2} \frac{\frac{\partial F(\bar{\eta})}{\partial s}}{g_1'(\bar{s})} \frac{k(\bar{\alpha} + b_1 \overline{\beta u}) h'(\bar{u})}{\left(wl_1 \overline{pu} + (\bar{\alpha} + b_1 \overline{\beta u}) + d_1 \right)} \quad (19.50)$$

Equation (19.50) is precisely (11.10).
This completes the proof of theorem 7.

19.12 Appendix 12. Proof of theorem 10

19.12.1 Linearization of the non linear system

As in appendix 19.13, (19.58) holds; moreover, since we are assuming null profit tax rate in $\bar{\eta} = (\bar{u}, \bar{s}, \bar{p}, \bar{z})$ (see (11.21)), it is clear from (11.19) that

$$\frac{\partial G(\bar{\eta})}{\partial s} = 0 \quad (19.51)$$

$$\frac{\partial G(\bar{\eta})}{\partial z} = 0,$$

while

$$\frac{\partial G\left(\bar{\eta}\right)}{\partial u} = -\frac{\overline{k}}{\overline{p}b_1}\left(\bar{\alpha} + b_1\bar{\beta}\bar{u}\right)\bar{h}'. \tag{19.52}$$

Thus the Jacobian matrix of the differential system (10.14) in each equilibrium point $\bar{\eta} = (\bar{u}, \bar{s}, \bar{p}, \bar{z})$ has the form

$$J = \begin{pmatrix} \dfrac{\partial F\left(\bar{\eta}\right)}{\partial u} & \dfrac{\partial F\left(\bar{\eta}\right)}{\partial s} & 0 & 0 \\[2ex] -\dfrac{\overline{k}}{\overline{p}b_1}\left(\bar{\alpha} + b_1\bar{\beta}\bar{u}\right)h'(\bar{u}) & 0 & \dfrac{\partial G\left(\bar{\eta}\right)}{\partial p} & 0 \\[2ex] 0 & \overline{p}\bar{g}_1' & 0 & 0 \\[2ex] \dfrac{\partial H\left(\bar{\eta}\right)}{\partial u} & \dfrac{\partial H\left(\bar{\eta}\right)}{\partial s} & \dfrac{\partial H\left(\bar{\eta}\right)}{\partial p} & \dfrac{\partial H\left(\bar{\eta}\right)}{\partial z} \end{pmatrix} ; \tag{19.53}$$

an elementary computation (see again (11.19)) yields

$$\frac{\partial G\left(\bar{\eta}\right)}{\partial p} = \frac{\vartheta'\left(\overline{p}_1\right)}{b_1\overline{p}_1} \tag{19.54}$$

$$\left[\left(b_1 - wl_1\right)\overline{pu} + \frac{b_2 - wl_2\overline{p}}{wl_2\overline{p}}\left(\bar{\alpha} + b_1\bar{\beta}\bar{u} - d_2\bar{z}\right) - \delta\bar{z}\right].$$

Substituting (11.23) into (19.54) and having in mind (19.58), it is easy to see that

$$\frac{\partial G\left(\bar{\eta}\right)}{\partial p} = \frac{\vartheta'\left(\overline{p}_1\right)}{b_1\overline{p}_1} \tag{19.55}$$

$$\left[\left(b_1 - wl_1\right)\overline{pu} + \frac{\left(b_2 - wl_2\overline{p}\right)\left(\bar{\alpha} + b_1\bar{\beta}\bar{u}\right)}{wl_2\overline{p}\left(\bar{\alpha} + b_1\bar{\beta}\bar{u}\right) + b_2d_2}\left(\bar{\alpha} + b_1\bar{\beta}\bar{u} - \delta + d_2\right)\right]$$

19.12.2 Characteristic polynomial

It is clear from (19.52) and (19.55) that $\frac{\partial G(\bar{\eta})}{\partial u} < 0$, while $\frac{\partial G(\bar{\eta})}{\partial p} > 0$; thus it is easy to see that the characteristic polynomial

$$P\left(\lambda\right) = \left(\lambda - \frac{\partial H\left(\bar{\eta}\right)}{\partial z}\right) \tag{19.56}$$

$$\left[\lambda^3 - \frac{\partial F\left(\bar{\eta}\right)}{\partial u}\lambda^2 - \left(\frac{\partial F\left(\bar{\eta}\right)}{\partial s}\frac{\partial G\left(\bar{\eta}\right)}{\partial u} + g_1'(\bar{s})\overline{p}\frac{\partial G\left(\bar{\eta}\right)}{\partial p}\right)\lambda + \right.$$

$$\left. g_1'(\bar{s})\overline{p}\frac{\partial G\left(\bar{\eta}\right)}{\partial p}\frac{\partial F\left(\bar{\eta}\right)}{\partial u}\right]$$

has a four roots with negative real part, provided that the coefficient of λ in the second factor of the right hand side of (19.56) is positive (see (19.48)).

This is the case if and only if

$$\vartheta'(\overline{p}_1) \;>\; \dfrac{\dfrac{\partial F(\bar{\eta})}{\partial s}}{g_1'(\bar{s})} \dfrac{1}{\overline{p}_2} \cdot \qquad (19.57)$$

$$\dfrac{\overline{k}\left(\bar{\alpha}+b_1\bar{\beta}\bar{u}\right)h'(\bar{u})}{(b_1-wl_1)\,\overline{pu}+\dfrac{(b_2-wl_2\overline{p})\left(\bar{\alpha}+b_1\bar{\beta}\bar{u}\right)}{wl_2\overline{p}\left(\bar{\alpha}+b_1\bar{\beta}\bar{u}\right)+b_2d_2}\left(\bar{\alpha}+b_1\bar{\beta}\bar{u}-\delta+d_2\right)}$$

This completes the proof of theorem 10.

19.13 Appendix 13. Proof of theorem 11

19.13.1 Linearization of the non linear system

We first notice that in each equilibrium point $\bar{\eta}$

$$\bar{\alpha}_{tp} \;=\; \bar{\alpha} \qquad (19.58)$$
$$\bar{\beta}_{tp} \;=\; \bar{\beta}$$

since we are assuming null profit tax rate there (see (11.24)). It is clear from (11.19) that

$$\dfrac{\partial G(\bar{\eta})}{\partial p} \;=\; 0 \qquad (19.59)$$
$$\dfrac{\partial G(\bar{\eta})}{\partial z} \;=\; 0,$$

while

$$\dfrac{\partial G(\bar{\eta})}{\partial u} = -\dfrac{\overline{k}}{\overline{p}b_1}\left(\bar{\alpha}+b_1\bar{\beta}\bar{u}\right)\bar{h}'. \qquad (19.60)$$

Thus the Jacobian matrix of the differential system (10.14) in each equilibrium point $\bar{\eta} = (\bar{u},\bar{s},\bar{p},\bar{z})$ has the form

$$J = \begin{pmatrix} \dfrac{\partial F(\bar{\eta})}{\partial u} & \dfrac{\partial F(\bar{\eta})}{\partial s} & 0 & 0 \\[2mm] -\dfrac{\overline{k}}{\overline{p}b_1}\left(\bar{\alpha}+b_1\bar{\beta}\bar{u}\right)h'(\bar{u}) & \dfrac{\partial G(\bar{\eta})}{\partial s} & 0 & 0 \\[2mm] 0 & \overline{p}\bar{g}_1' & 0 & 0 \\[2mm] \dfrac{\partial H(\bar{\eta})}{\partial u} & \dfrac{\partial H(\bar{\eta})}{\partial s} & \dfrac{\partial H(\bar{\eta})}{\partial p} & \dfrac{\partial H(\bar{\eta})}{\partial z} \end{pmatrix}; \quad (19.61)$$

an elementary computation (see again (11.19)) yields

$$\frac{\partial G\left(\bar{\eta}\right)}{\partial s} = \frac{\vartheta g_1'\left(\bar{s}\right)}{b_1 \bar{p}_1} \tag{19.62}$$

$$\left[\left(b_1 - wl_1\right)\overline{pu} + \frac{b_2 - wl_2\bar{p}}{wl_2\bar{p}}\left(\bar{\alpha} + b_1\bar{\beta}\bar{u} - d_2\bar{z}\right) - \delta\bar{z}\right].$$

Substituting (11.26) into (19.62) and having in mind (19.58), it is easy to see that

$$\frac{\partial G\left(\bar{\eta}\right)}{\partial s} = \frac{\vartheta g_1'\left(\bar{s}\right)}{b_1 \bar{p}_1} \tag{19.63}$$

$$\left[\left(b_1 - wl_1\right)\overline{pu} + \frac{\left(b_2 - wl_2\bar{p}\right)\left(\bar{\alpha} + b_1\bar{\beta}\bar{u}\right)}{wl_2\bar{p}\left(\bar{\alpha} + b_1\bar{\beta}\bar{u}\right) + b_2 d_2}\left(\bar{\alpha} + b_1\bar{\beta}\bar{u} - \delta + d_2\right)\right]$$

19.13.2   Characteristic polynomial

It is clear from (19.60) and (19.63) that $\frac{\partial G(\bar{\eta})}{\partial u} < 0$ and $\frac{\partial G(\bar{\eta})}{\partial s} < 0$; thus it is easy to see that the characteristic polynomial

$$P\left(\lambda\right) = \lambda\left(\lambda - \frac{\partial H\left(\bar{\eta}\right)}{\partial z}\right) \tag{19.64}$$

$$\left(\lambda^2 - \left(\frac{\partial F\left(\bar{\eta}\right)}{\partial u} + \frac{\partial G\left(\bar{\eta}\right)}{\partial s}\right)\lambda + \frac{\partial F\left(\bar{\eta}\right)}{\partial u}\frac{\partial G\left(\bar{\eta}\right)}{\partial s} - \frac{\partial F\left(\bar{\eta}\right)}{\partial s}\frac{\partial G\left(\bar{\eta}\right)}{\partial u}\right)$$

has a null root and three roots with negative real part if and only if the known term of the third factor of the right hand side of (19.64) is positive and this is the case if and only if

$$\vartheta > -\frac{\dfrac{\partial F\left(\bar{\eta}\right)}{\partial s}}{\dfrac{\partial F\left(\bar{\eta}\right)}{\partial u}}\frac{1}{g'\left(\bar{s}\right)} \tag{19.65}$$

$$\frac{\bar{k}\left(\bar{\alpha} + b_1\bar{\beta}\bar{u}\right)\bar{h}'}{\left(b_1 - wl_1\right)\overline{pu} + \dfrac{\left(b_2 - wl_2\bar{p}\right)\left(\bar{\alpha} + b_1\bar{\beta}\bar{u}\right)}{wl_2\bar{p}\left(\bar{\alpha} + b_1\bar{\beta}\bar{u}\right) + b_2 d_2}\left(\bar{\alpha} + b_1\bar{\beta}\bar{u} - \delta + d_2\right)}.$$

This completes the proof of theorem 11.

19.14   Appendix 14. Proof of theorem 14

19.14.1   Linearization an characteristic polynomial

We begin again deriving the function (12.24) in an equilibrium point $\bar{\eta} = \left(\bar{u}, \bar{s}, \bar{p}, \bar{z}\right)$.

$$\frac{\partial G\left(\bar{\eta}\right)}{\partial u} = -\frac{\bar{k}}{\bar{p}b_1}\left(\bar{\alpha}_{t^p} + b_1\bar{\beta}_{t^p}\bar{u}\right)h'(\bar{u}) + \tag{19.66}$$

$$\frac{1-\sigma}{\bar{p}b_1}\left[wl_1\bar{p} + b_1\bar{\beta}_{t^p} + \left(\bar{\alpha}_{t^p} + b_1\bar{\beta}_{t^p}\bar{u}\right)h'(\bar{u})\right],$$

$$\frac{\partial G\left(\bar{\eta}\right)}{\partial s} = -\frac{1-\sigma}{\bar{k}^2}\left[(b_1 - wl_1)\overline{pu} - d_1 - \delta\right] = -(1-\sigma)\frac{\overline{p}}{\bar{k}}, \tag{19.67}$$

$$\frac{\partial G\left(\bar{\eta}\right)}{\partial p} = 0, \tag{19.68}$$

$$\frac{\partial G\left(\bar{\eta}\right)}{\partial z} = 0. \tag{19.69}$$

Thus the Jacobian matrix of the differential system (11.14) in an equilibrium point $\bar{\eta}$ has again the form (19.61) and therefore the characteristic polynomial is given by (19.64)

These analogies with appendix 19.4 leads to an analogous conclusions since also now we have

$$\frac{\partial G\left(\bar{\eta}\right)}{\partial s} < 0. \tag{19.70}$$

Hence

$$-\left(\frac{\partial F\left(\bar{\eta}\right)}{\partial u} + \frac{\partial G\left(\bar{\eta}\right)}{\partial s}\right) > 0. \tag{19.71}$$

19.14.2 Sign of the eigenvalues

Thus the characteristic polynomial (19.64) has three negative roots with negative real part if and only if

$$\frac{\partial F\left(\bar{\eta}\right)}{\partial u}\frac{\partial G\left(\bar{\eta}\right)}{\partial s} - \frac{\partial F\left(\bar{\eta}\right)}{\partial s}\frac{\partial G\left(\bar{\eta}\right)}{\partial u} > 0. \tag{19.72}$$

An elementary computation shows that (19.72) yields (12.27).

Having in mind the economic meaning of σ, (12.27) makes sense if and only if $\sigma > 0$; this condition leads to the upper bound (12.25) on the accelerator with respect to the reactions of firms to stock and production disequilibrium.

20 List of Figures

21 List of Symbols

- B direct transfers to households, see subsections 9.1.2, 15.3.2

- $\overline{B}$ equilibrium value of the direct transfers to households, see subsections 9.1.2, 15.3.2

- B_U unemployment benefits, see subsections 12.2.2, 15.3.2

- $\widehat{B}$ matrix of the eigenvalues, see subsections 10.2.1, 19.4.1

- b_i marginal productivity of capital in sector i, see subsections 3.1.1, 14.1.1

- b_i^* marginal productivity of capital in sector i before the innovation, see subsections 7.2, 7.3, 7.4, 7.5

- C_i total (monetary) capital engaged in production in sector i, see subsection

- D_i aggregate demand for bundles of goods produced in sector i, see subsections 3.2.2, 3.3.1, 14.1.3

- D_T aggregate demand for consumption goods, see subsection 14.1.3

- d_i dividend paid by firms in sector i, see subsections 3.2.2, 3.3.1, 14.1.3

- d_i^{dit} dividend paid by firms in sector i, when there is a DIT, see subsection 9.4.1

- F evolution of the productive capacity utilization rate, see subsection 3.2.2

- G evolution of the inventory level, see section 5.1

- g_i rate of change of the price of goods produced in sector i, see subsections 3.2.1, 3.3.3

- H evolution of the relative capitalization z, see subsection 5.1

- h accelerator of the investment, see subsection 3.2.3

- I_i^a ex ante investment in sector i, see subsections 3.2.3, 14.1.2

- I_i investment in sector i, see subsections 3.1.2, 3.3.2, 3.3.3, 14.1.2

- I_i^n normal investment in sector i, see subsection 3.1.1

- J matrix of the linearized differential system, see subsection 19.3.1

- K_i stock of fixed capital engaged in production in sector i, see subsections 3.1.1, 14.1.1

- k_i money capita necessary to realize a unitary (fixed) investment in sector i, see subsections 3.1.2, 3.2.3, 3.3.3

- $\frac{l_i}{b_i}$ marginal productivity of labor in sector i, see subsections 3.1.1, 14.1.1

- $\frac{l_i^*}{b_i^*}$ marginal productivity of labor in sector i before the innovation, see subsections 7.2, 7.3, 7.4, 7.5

- L_i input of labor in sector i, see subsections 3.1.1, 3.2.1, 3.3.1, 14.1.1

- $\overline{L}_i$ normal employment level in sector i, see subsection 12.2.2

- P direct government purchases of goods and services, see subsection 9.1.2

- p_i unit price of the bundle of goods produced by firms in sector i, see subsections 3.2.1, 3.3.1, 14.1.1

- $p = \frac{p_1}{p_2}$ relative price, see subsection 4.1.1

- $\bar{p}$ equilibrium value of the relative price, see section 5.1

- $\overline{p^\nabla}$ equilibrium value for the relative price in the stationary disequilibrium case, see subsection 6.2.4

- r_i rate of profit for firms in sector i, see subsections 19.1.1, 19.1.2

- $\bar{r}_i$ equilibrium value of the rate of profit for firms in sector i, see subsections 19.1.1, 19.1.2

- r_i^* rate of profit for firms in sector i, before the innovation, see subsections 7.2, 7.3, 7.4, 7.5

- S_i inventories in sector i, see subsection 3.2.1

- s inventory level, see subsection 3.2.1

- $\bar{s}$ normal value of the inventory level, see subsection 3.2.1

- $\overline{s^\nabla}$ equilibrium value of the inventory level in the stationary disequilibrium case, see subsection 6.2.4

- T^p revenue of the profit tax, see subsection 9.1.1

- T^c revenue of the consumption tax, see subsection 9.1.3

- T^{dit} revenue of the DIT, see subsection 9.4.1

- t^p tax rate on profit, see subsection 9.1.1

- t^c tax rate on consumption expenditures, see subsection 9.1.3

- $\bar{t}^p$ equilibrium value of the tax rate on profits, see subsection 11.2.2

- $\bar{t}^c$ equilibrium value of the tax rate on consumption expenditures, see subsection 11.1.1

- $t^{p,1}$ tax rate on consumed profit, see subsection 9.4.1

- $t^{p,2}$ tax rate on reinvested profit, see subsection 9.4.1

- $\hat{t}_2$ point of the depression at which the capital goods sector looses its profitability, see subsection 6.1.1

- $\hat{t}_1$ point of the depression at which the consumption goods sector looses its profitability, see subsection 6.1.2

- $\hat{t}_0$ lower turning point, see subsection 6.1.3

- $\tilde{t}_3$ point of the expansion at which rationing of capital goods begins, see subsection 6.2.1

- $\tilde{t}_2$ point of the expansion at which the disequilibrium in profit rates ends, see subsection 6.2.2

- $\tilde{t}_1$ point of the expansion at which the disequilibrium in profit rates begins, see subsection 6.2.2

- $\tilde{t}$ upper turning point, see subsection 6.2.3

- U unemployment, see subsection 12.2.2

- u productive capacity utilization rate, see subsection 3.2.2

- $\bar{u}$ normal value of the productive capacity utilization rate, see subsection 3.2.2

- $\overline{u^\nabla}$ equilibrium value of the productive capacity utilization rate, in the stationary disequilibrium case, see subsection 6.2.4

- v_i eigenvector of the linearized system, see subsection 19.3.3

- W_i aggregate wage bill in sector i, see subsections 3.2.1, 3.3.1, 14.1.1

- w real wage rate (in the developed country), see subsection 3.2.1

- w_e real wage rate (in the developing country), see subsection 14.1.1

- Y_i output of firms in sector i, see subsections 3.1.1, 3.3.1, 3.3.2, 14.1.1

- $z = \frac{K_2}{K_1}$ relative capitalization of the second sector with respect to the first, see subsection 4.1.1

- $\bar{z}$ equilibrium value of the relative capitalization z, see section 5.1

- $\overline{z^\nabla}$ equilibrium value of the relative capitalization z, in the stationary disequilibrium case, see subsection 6.2.4

- $z_e = \frac{K_e}{K_1}$ relative capitalization of the new sector with respect to the first, see subsection 15.1.2

- α see subsection 4.1.1

- α_{t^p} see subsection 9.2.2

- α^{dit} see subsection 9.4.2

- β see subsection 4.1.1

- β_{t^p} see subsection 9.2.2

- β^{dit} see subsection 9.4.2

- γ see subsection 5.1

- δ depreciation rate of fixed capital, see subsection 3.2.1

- ε share of the aggregate demand satisfied by imported goods, see subsection 14.1.3

- ζ price gap between imported and domestically produced goods, see subsection 14.1.3

- $\eta = (u, s, p, z)$ vector of relative variables, see subsection 19.3.1

- $\overline{\eta} = (\overline{u}, \overline{s}, \overline{p}, \overline{z})$ equilibrium value of the vector of relative variables, see subsection 19.3.1

- ϑ variable part of the tax rate, see subsections 11.1.1, 11.1.2, 11.2.2, 11.2.3

- λ eigenvalue of the linearized system, see subsection 19.3.3

- Π_i (before tax) profit of firms in sector i, see subsections 3.2.2, 3.3.1, 14.1.1

- Π_i^a accumulated profit of firms in sector i, see subsections 3.1.2, 3.3.1, 14.1.1

- Π_i^c consumed profit of firms in sector i, see subsections 3.2.2, 3.3.1, 14.1.1

- Π_i^n after tax profit of firms in sector i, see subsection 9.1.1

- $\Pi_i^{a,n}$ after tax accumulated profit of firms in sector i, see subsections 9.4.1

- $\Pi_i^{c,n}$ after tax consumed profit of firms in sector i, see subsections 3.1.2, 3.3.1, 14.1.1

- ρ growth rate of the consumption goods sector, see subsection 4.1.1

- $\overline{\rho}$ equilibrium growth rate of the consumption goods sector, see section 5.1

- ρ_{tp} growth rate of the consumption goods sector, when the government levies a profit tax, see subsection 9.2.2

- ρ^{dit} growth rate of the consumption goods sector, when the government levies a DIT, see subsection 9.4.2

- σ part of income not covered by the unemployment benefit, see subsection 12.2.2

- $\overline{\sigma}$ upper bound for the part of income not covered by the unemployment benefit, see subsection 12.2.4

References

[1] Aftalion, A. (1913): *Les crises periodiques de surproduction.* **Marcel Riviere**, Paris.

[2] Aftalion, A. (1927): Theory of Economic Cycles Based on the Capitalistic Technique of Production. *The Review of Economic Statistics* **9**, 165-170.

[3] Aoki, M. (1977): Dual Stability in a Cambridge-Type Model. *The Review of Economic Studies* **44**, 143-151.

[4] Arrow, K. J.; Karling, ; Scarf, (1958): *Studies in the Mathematical Theory of Inventory and Production* **Stanford University Press**, Stanford.

[5] Arrow, K. J. (1962): The Economic Implications of Learning by Doing. *Review of Economic Studies* **29**, 155-173.

[6] Asada, T. (1987): Government Finance and Wealth effect in a Kaldorian Cycle Model. *Journal of Economics* **47**, 143-166.

[7] Aschauer, K. (1988): *Does Public Capital Crowd Out Private Capital?* **Federal Reserve Bank of Chicago.**

[8] Barnett, W. A.; Geweke, J.; Shell, K. eds.(1994): *Economic Complexity: Chaos, Sunspots, Bubbles, and Nonlinearity.***Cambridge University Press**, Cambridge.

[9] Belloc, B. (1980): *Croissance economique et adaptation du capital productif* **Economica,** Paris.

[10] Benhabib, J. ed. (1992): *Cycles and Chaos in Economic Equilibrium* **Princeton University Press**, Princeton NJ.

[11] Benhabib, J.; Nishimura, K.(1979): The Hopf Bifurcation and the Existence and Stability of Closed Orbits in Multisector Models of Optimal Growth. *Journal of Economic Theory* **21**, 421-444.

[12] Blinder, A.; Solow, R. (1973): Does Fiscal Policy Matter? *Journal of Public Economics* **2**, 37-44.

[13] Bliss, C. J. (1968): On Putty-Clay, *The Review of Economic Studies* **35** (2), 105-135.

[14] Boggio, L. (1993): Production Prices and Dynamic Stability: Results and Open Questions, *Manchester School* **XV**, 264-294.

[15] Boggio, L. (1993): On Local Relative Stability with Special Reference to Economic Applications, *Rivista di Matematica per le Scienze Economiche e Sociali* **16**, 3-16.

[16] Boggio, L.; Gozzi, G. C. (1993): La stabilità dei prezzi di produzione. in Zaghini (1993).

[17] Bouniatin, M. (1922): *Les Crises Economiques* **M. Girard**, Paris.

[18] Bresciani-Turroni, C. (1936): The Theory of Saving II *Economica* **16**, 162-181.

[19] Burmeister, E.; Dobell, A. R. (1970): *Mathematical Theory of Economic Growth.* **Macmillan**, London.

[20] Burmeister, E.; Caton, C.; Dobell, A. R.; Ross, S. (1973): The "Saddle-point Property" and the Structure of Dynamic Heterogeneous Capital Good Models. *Econometrica* **41**, 79-95.

[21] Burmeister, E. (1980): *Capital Theory and Dynamics,* **Cambridge University Press**, Cambridge.

[22] Cantalupi, M.; Nardini, F.; Ricottilli, M. (1992): A Development Strategy with Foreign Borrowing: a Neo-Austrian Approach. *Structural Change and Economic Dynamic* **3**, 201-221.

[23] Cass, D.; Shell, K. (1976): Introduction to Hamiltonian Dynamics in Economics. *Journal of Economic Theory* **12**, 1-10.

[24] Chang, W.; Smith, D. (1971): The Existence and Persistence of Cycles in a non Linear Model: Kaldor's 1940 Model Re-Examined. *The Review of Economic Studies* **38**, 37-44.

[25] Day, R. (1984): *Adaptive Disequilibrium Dynamics of Urban-Regional Development.* **The Netherland Institute for Advanced Studies,** Wassenaar.

[26] Delli Gatti, D.; Gallegati, M. (1991): Credito, investimenti e fluttuazioni economiche. l'economia "sequenziale" di Marco Fanno. *Quaderni di Storia dell'Economia Politica,* **IX**, 1.

[27] Dixit, A. K.. (1976): The Theory of Equilibrium Growth. **Oxford University Press,** Oxford..

[28] Dixit, A. K.; Pindyck, R. S. (1994): Investment under Uncertainty. **Princeton University Press,** Princeton NJ.

[29] Duménil, G.; Lévy, D. (1989): The Competitive Process in a Fixed Capital Environment: a Classical View. *The Manchester School* **62**, 34-57.

[30] Duménil, G.; Lévy, D. (1993): *The Economics of the Profit Rate.* **Edward Elgar.**

[31] Evans, G.; Honkapoja, S.; Romer, P. (1998): Growth Cycles. Preprint **AER.**

[32] Faber, M.; Proops, J. L. R. (1990): *Evolution, Time, Production, and the Environment.* **Springer Verlag,** Berlin.

[33] Fanno, M. (1931): Cicli di produzione e cicli del credito. *Giornale degli Economisti ed Annali di Economia* (English version published in *Structural Change and Economic Dynamics* **4**, 403-437).

[34] Gomulka, S. (1986): Soviet Growth Slowdown: Duality, Maturity, and Innovation. *The Economic Journal* **76**, 170-174.

[35] Goodwin, R. M. (1951): The Non Linear Accelerator and the Persistence of Business Cycle. *Econometrica* **19**, 1-17.

[36] Goodwin, R. M. (1967): A Growth Cycle, in *Socialism, Capitalism and Economic Growth,* Feinstein, C. H. ed. **Cambridge University Press,** Cambridge.

[37] Goodwin, R. M. (1982): *Essays in Linear Economic Structures,* **Macmillan,** London..

[38] Gozzi; G., Nardini, F. (2000): A Two-sector Model of the Business Cycle: a Prototype Analysis *Working Paper Dipartimento di Scienze Economiche di Bologna* , Bologna.

[39] Grandmont, J. M. (1985): On Endogenous Competitive Business Cycles. *Econometrica* **53**, 995-1045.

[40] Hagemann, H.; Gehrke H. (1996): Efficient Traverse and Bottlenecks, in *Production and Economic Analysis*. Landesmann M., Scazzieri R. eds., **Cambridge University Press**, Cambridge.

[41] Hagemann, H.; Hamouda, O. eds. (1992): *The Legacy of Hicks* **Routledge**, London..

[42] Hagemann, H.; Kurz, H. D. eds. (1998): *Political Economics in Retrospect. Essays in Memory of Adolph Lowe.* **Edward Elgar**, Chentelham.

[43] Hagemann, H.; Landesmann, M. (1998): *Lowe and Structurel Theories of the Business Cycle.* in [42].

[44] Hahn, F. H. (1966): Equilibrium Dynamics with Heterogeneuos Capital Goods, *Quarterly Journal of Economics* **80**, 633-646.

[45] Haken, H. (1977): *Synergetics: an Introduction.* **Springer Verlag**, Berlin.

[46] Haken, H. (1983): *Advanced Synergetics.* **Springer Verlag**, Berlin.

[47] Hicks, J. (1950): *A Contribution to the Theory of Trade Cycle.* **Clarendon Press**, Oxford.

[48] Hicks, J. (1965): *Capital and Growth.* **Oxford University Press**, Oxford.

[49] Hicks, J. (1973): *Capital and Time: a Neo-Austrian Theory.* **Oxford University Press**, Oxford.

[50] Hicks, J. (1974): *Crises in Keynesian Economics.* **Basil Blackwell**, Oxford.

[51] Hicks, J. (1984): *Methods of Dynamic Economics.***Oxford University Press**, Oxford.

[52] Hicks, J. (1989): *A Market Theory of Money.* **Clarendon Press**, Oxford.

[53] Holt, C.C.; Modigliani, F.; Muth, J.M.; Simon, H.A. (1960): *Planning Production Inventories and Work Force* **Prentice Hall**, New York.

[54] Jorgenson, J. (1961): A Dual Stability Theory. *Econometrica* **28**, 892-899.

[55] Judd, K. L.; Petersen, B. C. (1986): Dynamic limit pricing and internal finance. *Journal of Economic Theory.*

[56] Kaldor, N.: (1940): A Model of Trade Cycle. *Economic Journal* **50**, 78-92.

[57] Klamer, A.; Mc Closkey, D. (1992): Accounting as the Master Metaphor of Economics. *The European Accounting Review,* **1**.

[58] Kuga, M. (1977): General Saddlepoint Property of the Steady State of a Growth Model with Heterogeneous Capital Goods. *International Economic Review* **18**, 209-225.

[59] Kurz, M. (1968): The General Instability of a Close Competitive Growth Process. *Review of Economic Studies,* **35**, 155-174.

[60] Lorenz, H. W. (1987): Multisector Model of Trade Cycle. *Journal of Economic Behaviour and Organization* **8** (3)**,** 397-412.

[61] Lowe, A.. (1976): *The path of economic growth,* **Cambridge University Press**, Cambridge.

[62] Magnan de Bornier, J. (1980): *Economie de la traverse.. Essai d'-analyse dans un cadre néo-autrichien.* Economica, Paris.

[63] Meade, J. (1961): *A Neoclassical Theory of Growth.* **Allen & Unwin**, London.

[64] Morishima, M. (1964): *Equilibrium Stability and Growth.* **Oxford University Press**, Oxford.

[65] Morishima, M. (1969): *Theory of Economic Growth.* **Clarendon Press**, Oxford.

[66] Nardini, F. (1990): Cycle-Trend Dynamics in a Fixwage Neo-Austrian Model of Traverse. *Structural Change and Economic Dynamics* **1** (1), 165-194.

[67] Nardini, F. (1994): Delayed Response to Shocks in the Neo-Austrian Model: Characteristics of the Traverse Path. *Metroeconomica* **45** (1), 17-46.

[68] Nishimura, K.; Jano, M. (1994): Non Linearity and Business Cycles in a Two-Sectors Equilibrium Model: an Example with Cobb-Douglas Production Function, *Ricerche Economiche* **48** , 185-199.

[69] Nishimura, K.; Jano, M. (1995)a: Dynamic and Chaos in Optimal Growth: an Example, *Econometrica* **63** (4), 981-1001.

[70] Nishimura, K.; Jano, M. (1995)b: Durable Capital and Chaos in Competitive Business Cycles, *Journal of Economic Behaviuor and Organization* **27** (2), 165-181.

[71] Pasinetti, L. (1965): *A Multisector model of Economic Growth.* **Cambridge University Press**, Cambridge.

[72] Pasinetti, L. (1981): *Structural Change and Economic Growth.* **Cambridge University Press**, Cambridge.

[73] Pasinetti, L. (1993): *Structural Economic Dynamics.* **Cambridge University Press**, Cambridge.

[74] Phelp, E. S.(1995): *Structural Slumps: the Modern Equilibrium Theory of Unemployment, Intereset, and Assets.* **Harward University Press**.

[75] Ricardo, D. (1817): *The Principles of Political Economy and Taxation.* **Dent & Son Ttd.** , London 1960.

[76] Rosenberg, N. (1982): *Inside the Black Box. Technology and Economics.* **Cambridge University Press** , Cambridge.

[77] Samuelson, P. (1962): Parable and Realism in a Capital Theory: the Surrogate Production Function. *Review of Economic Studies* **30**, 193-206.

[78] Scazzieri, R. (1992): Economic Theory and Economic History: Perspectives on Hiksian Themes. in [41].

[79] Solow, R. M. (1965): A contribution to the Theory of Economic Growth. *Quarterly Juornal of Economics,* **70**, 65-94.

[80] Solow R.; Tobin, J.; Von Weizsäcker, C.C.; Yaari, M. (1966): Neoclassical Growth with Fixed Factor Proportions, *The Review of Economic Studies* **33** (2), 79-115.

[81] Spiethoff, A.(1925): Krisen, in *Handwoerterbuch der Staatswiessenschaften,* **VI**, 8-91.

[82] Swan, T. (1956): Economic Growth and Capital Accumulation. *Economic Record,* **32**, 334-361.

[83] Tugan Baranowskj: (1901), *Studien zur Theorie und Geschichte der Handelskrisen in England,* Gustav Fischer, Jena. (translation of *Promylshennye krizisy v sovremennoi Anglii.* St. Petersburg (1894)).

[84] Uzawa H. (1961): On a Two Sectors Model of Economic Growth: I, *Review of Economic Studies* **29**, 40-47.

[85] Vianello, F. (1985): The Pace of Accumulation. *Political Economy* **7**.

[86] Woodford, M. (1994): Imperfect Financial Intermediation and Complex Dynamics, in *Economic Complexity: Chaos, Sunspots, Bubbles, and Nonlinearity.* Barnett, W. A.; Geweke, J.; Shell, K. eds. **Cambridge University Press**, Cambridge.

[87] Woodford, M. (1990): Equilibrium Models with Endogenous Fluctuations: an Introduction. Working Paper No. 3360, **National Bureau of Economic Research, Inc.**, Cambridge MA.

[88] Zaghini, C. (1993): *Economia matematica. Equilibri e dinamica.* **UTET**, Torino.

[89] Zamagni, S. (1984): Ricardo and Hayek Effect in a Fixwage Model of Traverse. *Oxford Economic Papers* **36**, 135-151.

[90] Zhang, W. B. (1991): *Synergetic Economics: Time and Change in Nonlinear Economics,* **Springer Verlag**, Berlin.

Printing: Weihert-Druck GmbH, Darmstadt
Binding: Buchbinderei Schäffer, Grünstadt